OLD BRAY
AND ITS
NEIGHBOURHOOD

Some forgotten stories about the
'Gateway to the Garden of Ireland'

OLD BRAY
AND ITS NEIGHBOURHOOD

by
Francis Loughrey

Published in Ireland 1998

British Library Cataloguing in Publication Data.

A catalogue record of this book is available from the British Library.

ISBN 0 9520106 1 5

FOREWORD

This little volume has no pretensions about being a learned record of 'History'. It is a collection of my thoughts on places in Bray and the surrounding areas and of events that occurred there in the dim and distant past. Perhaps it will bring back to you dreams and memories and give you some little pleasure when you rest alone and listen to the silence.

Dedicated to my wife and friend Dymphna.

Francis Loughrey 1998

CONTENTS

Illustrations

SMUGGLERS

What could be a better way to commence *Old Bray and its Neighbourhood* than with an account of what transpired there many, many, decades ago. You've heard of Hastings, on the south east coast of Sussex in England, where smugglers thrived and fierce battles were fought between them and the Preventative Men. Well here in Bray similar activity occurred, but unlike Hastings where the caves were situated a long and strenuous walk from the beach, our cave was on the water line and was known as The Brandy Hole. Close by here, in the 18th century, there were only two dwellings. One was a make-shift hovel and referred to by locals as 'the Rat Hole'. To know that you were close to this didn't require the use of your eyes because a blind person would be well aware that it was there due to the dreadful sickening and nauseating smell that wafted through the air surrounding it. Rotten vegetation, stinking seaweed, worm crawling meat, maggoty infested stale fish, a never emptied cess pit and anything that gave off an abominable unclean stink was spread around it in great heaps. A veritable feast for bluebottles and big fattening chandlers. Within dwelt an ancient and eccentric fisherman whose seafaring days were over, who took great delight in collecting this refuse and who could sometimes be seen sniffing and rubbing it on his nostrils with a smile of ecstatic pleasure on his face as if what he had were the greatest and sweetest aromas from the orient.

The other, a well-constructed, humble yet comfortable building, was the home of a widow woman and her grown-up daughter both of whom appeared to make their living by gathering the small coloured stones from the beach which they would polish and sell to visitors. An honest and safe way to earn a livelihood but not greatly profitable. She also had another job which was secretive, dangerous and very, very profitable. The widow was in cahoots with the many smugglers and was an agent employed by them for the distribution of contraband as well as acting as a reliable informant and lookout on the movement of the Preventative Men. This woman, it is said, took part in the many fracas that occurred at night and she was no mean adversary. Being always armed with a musket and sabre she was the match of any man. When she died her daughter discovered that she was worth a fortune, as she was the surprised heir to real estate and boxes of gold sovereigns that made her wealthy for the remainder of her days.

Now you may be thinking that such activity was looked upon in those times as evil, but a reference to such activity was described in a church notice over a century ago "smuggling at the period of which we write, was not looked upon in the same light as it is at the present day, in fact it was secretly encouraged by many, even by those in the higher walks of life and numerous cases of wine, silks, brocades and foreign produce generally, found eager purchasers, as cheating His then Majesty's Revenue was most leniently looked upon by them and, if a sin, one of the most venial character."

Shortly after the death of the widow woman and the poor wretch that lived in the 'Rat Hole', around about the year 1825, there was a family named Byrne living at the western slope of the Head. Old Byrne, who in his younger days, was a fisherman and now was a successful farmer, his wife, two sons and daughter, Moya, all lived happily together. Moya was pretty and was "just verging from the blushing laughing-eyed girl into the more matured charms of womanhood". On visiting Bray's Main Street from time to time, while going on errands shopping for her mother, she became friendly with a young man named Garret O'Toole, whose father and mother had died of the 'fever' when he was a child. A relative kindly took on the position of foster parent and taught him about farming as well as providing him with a good education. Garret, as he grew older, felt that he was a burden to his kind kinsman and eagerly sought employment so that he might become independent.

One day, while walking on the strand aimlessly throwing stones into the water, he was approached by a sailor who asked him if he would like a job. It was

Bray Head and Beach

7

obvious to Garret that the stranger was an 'old salt' from the way he was attired. Garret readily agreed to perform whatever task was asked of him and he was immediately employed unloading a cargo of contraband from a vessel anchored off Bray Head. He was well rewarded for his services and from then on he was regularly employed in the activity of smuggling.

The friendship between Moya and Garret grew stronger until Moya decided that it was time that her father and mother were informed of their attachment to one another. She asked her mother to broach the subject with her father. When her father heard of the matter he ranted and raved and wouldn't give his consent to the friendship of the two young people developing any further. According to him Garret was nothing but a common smuggler without any hope of leading a successful life; the young man would end up at the end of a rope. His wife pleaded Garret's cause but without any success. Moya, being a dutiful and obedient daughter, promised her father that she would not introduce the subject again and that she would refrain from having any meetings with Garret

On hearing this bad news Garret resolved to change his employment so that he might continue his friendship with Moya and be accepted with favour by her father. He had a substantial sum of money saved and with it he purchased some land, in Little Bray beside the Dargle, which he commenced to farm. Soon he was earning as much as he had been making from smuggling and it was inevitable that he was to meet Moya, by chance, Bray being such a small place. When they both renewed their friendship the young couple agreed that the time was ripe for another attempt to obtain the goodwill and the blessing of Moya's father.

A few evenings later the young man presented himself at his intended's home where he explained his changed and successful way of life to her father. Instead of being received with kindness and civility, poor O'Toole was chastised and ridiculed and the mother and father of a row ensued. He was ordered to leave the house, never to darken its door again, and angry words were exchanged aloud between them both.

Subsequently, the same night, the old man went out for a breath of fresh air to cool his temper and perhaps to ponder on what had transpired. Had he acted too hastily? Was his decision a wrong one ? Was he breaking his daughter's heart? These thoughts were running through his troubled mind as he went towards the cliff walk that goes around Bray Head. That was the last time he was seen alive. When he failed to return to his home that night his family set out to search for him without success. The following morning, when the dawn had brightened up the day, his broken body was found lying above the high water mark beneath the cliff.

Foul play was immediately suspected and Garret was apprehended and committed to gaol where his trial was set for the following month at the assizes at Wicklow. All the evidence was against him. Moya and her mother were called to testify and under cross examination they tearfully described what had transpired on that fateful evening. The row, the angry words, the heated arguments between both. Neighbours who were within hearing on that night were also examined and they, too, bore witness to what was said. Both Moya and her mother also told the judge that they believed that Garret could never have committed such a crime. All the evidence was against him and the jury quickly returned a verdict of guilty. The judge was in the process of delivering the awful sentence of death when there was a commotion at the entrance of the court. Silence was ordered without any effect and into the body of the chamber came several fierce looking seamen one of whom stated that he was spokesman for the group.

It transpired from the leader's evidence that they were all Arklow fishermen and that they were off Bray Head on the fateful night in question. They described the evening being a bright moonlight one and while they were hauling their nets they saw Mr. Byrne, whom they knew quite well, on the cliff path. He appeared to be agitated so they shouted at him to mind his step as he was seen stumbling a little but he didn't seem to heed them. They debated among themselves as to whether they should send one of their members ashore to give him assistance but on looking again they saw that he had recovered his equilibrium. There was no other person near him and they lost sight of him and assumed that he was safe. They now believed that he had again tripped and fallen over the precipice. It was only lately that they had heard of the trial and had rushed to the court to give evidence in order to save the life of an innocent man.

The judge asked that all the seamen be sworn in and each testified to the truth of their leader's statement. Garret was immediately pronounced not guilty and the resounding cheers of all present signified their unanimous approval.

Garret and Moya, after a respectable period of mourning, resumed their friendship and were eventually married in Holy Redeemer Church and they lived happily ever after.

It is more than likely that the sailors, who came to Garret's defence in the court, were engaged in the trade of smuggling as Arklow fishermen would rarely, if ever, be fishing at night so near in to Bray Head and especially so close that they could recognise someone walking on the path. Smuggling continued in Bray up to the coming of the railway in 1854 and the use of the Brandy Hole was no longer possible as the passage to it was destroyed when the track was laid.

There was a silent witness to all that had happened here through the long centuries - the ruin of the little church that still stands on the northern slope of Bray Head, Raheenacluig, commanding awesome panoramic views of Bray and the area that lies to the north. The peace and the solitude which prevails here is indicative of its hallowed past. In the sky above the venerable stones there once flew golden eagles, peregrine falcons, ravens, short-eared owls, buzzards and merlins. To-day there remain many species of bird and animal life which are worth studying.

Raheenacluig

This little ruined picturesque shrine is easily accessible for the less energetic, being just a hundred yards above the car park and situated in the middle of a small eighteen hole golf course. Its history is somewhat obscure. Dr. Donnelly, parish priest of Bray, wrote about it in 1898 and gave us a description of what it was like then as well as recording the folklore and tradition associated with it.

The name in English translates as The Little Rath of the Bell. (As a matter of interest there is a bell on display in the Hunt Museum, Limerick, known as The Bray Bell.) There is now no sign of the belfry where the bell hung. This little bell is indicated on our municipal armorial bearings*. There were two smaller buildings near the east side of the church but now no trace of these exist. Twenty eight paces south east there was a piece of ground enclosed by a trench and a low mound sixty paces long by twelve wide and in 1898 there were two stones which marked the entrance to this site. It was supposed that this was the cemetery and people then remembered that unbaptised children were buried there. A few centuries ago there was a rough road leading from the church through the grounds of Presentation College (then the estate of the Putlands) and around the year 1780, long after signs of this track had disappeared and been forgotten, Edwards of Oldcourt Castle was clearing a hedge to make way for another carriageway when the workmen discovered a granite pedestal with ancient markings on it. Major Edwards had the stone moved to his residence. The workmen employed believed the cross that once stood on the pedestal was still there in the hedge, perhaps it still is.

Much of what was here in the past is gone forever, destroyed by ignorance, by the bulldozers or diggers that levelled the ground to make way for the little golf course. The bones of the little children that once lay here are scattered and dumped in many obscure and never to be discovered unconsecrated holes.

Beneath Bray's Towering craggy head,
Rest the windswept ruined hallowed stones
That once sheltered the tiny bones
Of innocent babes long, long dead.
Interred in ancient holy ground,
Without the sound of a funeral bell,
No hymns, priests prayers or mournful knell,
But the caoining and cry of seabird sound.
On grassy slope with aspect fair,
Sanctified and blessed by mothers tears,
Their nightmares realised, awful fears
Confirmed, nothing now but deep despair.
Angel souls not to heaven bound,
But into Limbo, so we were told
By teachers in foolish days of old,
These unbaptised babes were to be found.
For them no funeral Mass was said,
Just a plot of ground in some penal day
Beside that little rath at Bray.
No mark or record where they were laid
In earth forgotten and yet blessed,
Where once eagle, falcon and raven fly,

Singing a sad lament, no lullaby,
Their tiny corpses uncaressed.
Raheenacluig, lonely and forlorn,
No history, no memory now recalls
What once occurred outside its walls;
Babes all un-named, no one to mourn.

* *The Armorial Bearings also contain a lion, which represents the arms of the O'Tooles, who once owned all the land of Powerscourt and much of the area around Bray, a mermaid, which is on the arms of the O'Byrnes, who also controlled much of the territory and whose lands were also confiscated, and a martlet (heraldic swallow), on the arms and this represents the Brabazons whose descendants are the Earls of Meath. In the centre there is a chevron 'rompu' which represents the bridge (built by David Edge in 1856) over the Dargle river (recently damaged by a heavy vehicle and repaired in a rudely unsatisfactory way).*

THE KILRUDDERY HUNT

I have often heard of the Kilruddery Hunt but, thankfully, I've never seen the sad spectacle. My sympathy, and I believe that of many of my readers is with the fox and a happy ending to a story of the hunt is always when Reynard 'goes to earth'. I believe that it's right for a farmer to kill an animal that is destroying his stock but the idea of gentlemen ruffians on horses killing for sport appals me.

The song was written by one, Thomas Mozeen, who was a regular patron of a famous hostelry at Loughlinstown. The pub was situated opposite to Loughlinstown House and was demolished to make way for Beechwood. Shortly after its composition it became the most popular piece of music to be played in Bray and the surrounding countryside.

The Kilruddery Hunt

Hark ! Hark ! jolly sportsmen, awhile to my tale,
Which to pay attention I'm sure cannot fail;
'Tis of lads and of horses, and dogs that ne're tire,
O'er stone walls and hedges, through dale, bog and briar;
A pack of such hounds and a set of such men,
'Tis a shrewd chance if ever you meet with again;
Had Nimrod, the mightiest of hunters, been there,
'Fore God, he had shook like an aspen for fear.

In seventeen hundred and forty four,
The fifth of December, I think 'twas no more,
At five in the morning by most of the clocks,
We rode from Kilruddery in search of a fox.
The Loughlinstown landlord, the brave Owen Bray,
And Johnny Adair, too, were with us that day;
Joe Debil, Hal Preston - those huntsmen so stout-
Dick Holmes, some few others, and so we set out.

We cast off our hounds for a full hour or more,
When Wanton set up a most terrible roar,
'Hark to Wanton!' cried Joe, and the rest were not slack,
For Wanton's no trifler esteemed in the pack.
Old Bonny and Collier came readily in,
And every hound joined in the musical din;

Had Diana been there, she'd been pleased to the life,
And one of the lads got a goddess to wife.
Ten minutes past nine was the time of the day,
When Reynard broke cover, and this was his way;
As strong from Killegar as if he could fear none,
Away he brushed round by the house of Kilternan;
To Carrickmines thence, and to Cherrywood then,
Steep Shankill he climbed, and to Ballyman Glen;
Bray Common he crossed, leaped Lord Anglesea's wall,
And seemed to say ' Little I care for you all.'

He ran Bushe's Grove up to Carbury Byrne's -
Joe Debil, Hal Preston, kept leading by turns;
The earth it was open, yet he was so stout,
Though he might have got in, still he chose to keep out.
To Malpas high hill was the way that he flew ;
At Dalkey Stone Common we had him in view ;
He drove on by Bullock , through Shrub Glenageary,
And so on the Monkstown where Larry grew weary.

Through Rochestown wood like an arrow he passed,
And came to the steep hill of Dalkey at last;
There gallantly plunged himself into the sea,
And said in his heart,' None can now follow me.'
But soon to his cost, he perceived that no bounds
Could stop the pursuit of the staunch - mettled hounds;
His policy here did not serve him a rush,
Five couple of Tartars were here at his brush.

To recover the shore then again was his drift;
But ere he could reach to the top of the clift,
He found both of speed and of daring a lack,
Being waylaid and killed by the rest of the pack.
At his death there were present the lads I have sung,
Save Larry who, riding a garron was flung,
Thus ended at length a most delicate chase,
That held us for five hours and ten minutes space.

We returned to Kilruddery's plentiful board,
Where dwell hospitality, truth and my lord;

We talked o'er the chase and we toasted the health
Of the men who ne'er struggled for places or wealth.
Owen Bray baulked a leap - says Hal Preston 'Twas odd,'
'Twas shameful,' cried Hal, ' by the great living —'
Said Preston, I haloo'd 'Get on though you fall'
Or I'll leap over you, your blind gelding and all.'

Each glass was adapted to freedom and sport,
For party affairs were consigned to the Court;
Thus we finished the rest of the day and the night,
In gay flowing bumpers and toasts of delight.
Then till the next meeting, bade farewell to each brother-
So some they went one way, and some went another;
And as Phoebus befriended our earlier roam,
So Luna took care in conducting us home.

Bonny, Wanton, Collier: *Hounds in the Earl of Meath's pack;* **Killegar:** *Townland west of the Scalp;* **Steep Shankill:** *Carrickgollogan Mountain (Katy Gallagher's hostelry in Bray gets its name from this);* **Carbury Byrne's:** *a house in Cabinteely;* **Malpas high hill:** *Killiney Hill (Colonel Malpas erected the prominent obelisk);* **Garron :** *a nag .* **Kilruddery :** *Seat of the Earls of Meath (Brabazons).*

and for those who wish to play the music here is the score :

The Kilruddery Hunt

BRAY'S CATHOLIC PAST

No narrative about Bray can be complete without mention of Holy Redeemer Church on the Main Street with its very Irish, and unique-looking architectural front and with what I have come to describe as a Saint Catherine window dominating the view from the Florence Road. The architect responsible for this pleasing sight was Mr. Brendan Ellis who, because of his many ecclesiastical works, was decorated by the late Pope with the order of Knight of Saint Gregory. It's a suitable and interesting subject to commence our rambles and musings.

Most people think that the history of this church goes back to 1792 and they would be forgiven for this as the available records, preserved in the sacristy, date from then. Indeed it was only a few years ago that there were the Bi-centenary celebrations. Visitors find the building confusing because of its different architecture and furnishings and I will attempt to throw some light on to this by going back to where I believe it all started. It is also the time when Bray was in its infancy.

In or about the year 1630, during the reign of Charles 1st, a Father Dermot Byrne was parish priest of Bray and Kilmacanogue and it's recorded that he celebrated Mass in private houses at Oldcourt and Kilmacanogue. Terrible persecution of Catholics prevailed in those dark days and no Catholic places of worship were allowed. Just before Father Byrne arrived there was an account of what it was like in Bray and Enniskerry left to us by a Jesuit priest in 1619:

> the southern part of the Diocese of Dublin, possessed by a recent colony of English Protestant settlers who forbid any priest to approach that region . . . the Catholics there were reduced to extreme penury under these cruel masters, and though most tenacious of the faith, they had not the consolation of religion when they were dying; and those who were courageous and strong had to go out by night and come home the same night, when desirous of going to confession. When women were about to give birth to children, under pretence of going to relations or friends, they went to a neighbouring or distant district in order that the new-born babes might be baptised by a priest.

> In times past one of our fathers managed to give some spiritual help. This year about the feast of the Assumption, he remained with them a month hearing confessions, instructing them day and night. Crowds came to him, the sick were brought in carts, some not able to travel were carried on the shoulders of their neighbours, some remained for

four or five days in one place waiting their turn to go to confession; seven hundred went to the sacraments.

Father Byrne was parish priest until 1649 or 1650, when, as recorded by Bishop Donnelly, who was PP at the close of the nineteenth century. "Cromwell's curse fell upon the country". Cromwell passed through Bray on his way to massacre the people in Wexford town. This period is dark and obscure in our history and we are not aware of the name of any parish priest or indeed even curate for the next forty years.

In 1690 Father Richard Fitzsimons, who lived in Kilmacanogue, was appointed. There was a new law introduced in 1704 whereby all priests had to be registered, that no bishops, vicar generals or members of orders were to be allowed into the kingdom under penalty of high treason, one priest was allowed to each parish but he was to have no successor, so that at his death Catholic worship in that parish would cease. Under this act Father Fitzsimons registered as follows :

Richard Fitzsimons, living at Kilmullen age 46. Parish priest of Delgany, Powerscourt, Kilmacanogue and Bray. Ordained 1682 in Flanders by the Archbishop of Cambray. Sureties, Peter White, Wicklow; Matthew Robinet, Wicklow. in £50 each.

Father Fitzsimons survived until about 1740 and was succeeded by Rev. Stephen Cavenagh until 1747 when he was transferred to Wicklow where he died in 1753. He left a will whilst he was here which read:

In the name of God, Amen. I, Stephen Cavenagh bequeath to Anne Burke, Edmund Burke's wife, of Kilmurry, Parish of Kilmacanogue, one silver cup with my name inscribed. To Walter Byrne of Killoughter, one silver cup with William Cavenagh's name. To John Burke, son of Edmund, my hat, wig, slieve buttons and knee buckles. To Patrick Byrne of the Downs, parish of Kilcoole, a press. Horse and watch to be sold to defray funeral expenses. Executors. Witnesses Patrick Fitzsimons and Val. Burke, 23rd February, 1747.

After Canon Cavenagh's transfer to Wicklow town there is a gap in our records for ten years. There was, without doubt, another parish priest but his name is obscured by the difficulties of those sad times. The next we know about is Father Arthur O'Neill who was here from 1760 until 1794. (As a matter of interest there is, in the sacristy, a chalice dated 1769). The approximate population then was 2,177 broken down by area in the parish as Bray 400; Kilmacanogue 570 and Powerscourt 1,200.

17

FATHER CHRISTOPHER CALLAGHAN

During Father O'Neill's time his curate was Father Christopher Callaghan who arrived in Bray in 1792 and it is from this date that he recorded baptisms and marriages in the registers that are still preserved to-day in the church. When Father O'Neill died Father Callaghan succeeded him as parish priest. He studied in Paris and returned to Ireland in 1785.

He wasn't long here when the rising of 1798 broke out and Bishop Nicholas Donnelly notes "The '98 rebellion was the troubled time of the new pastor's administration. No parish in Wicklow was free from its influence or from the terrible vengeance that followed in its track". Many of the priests in Wicklow and Wexford were killed and it is likely that Father Callaghan would have shared the same fate but for the kindness of the Earl of Meath who gave him sanctuary and allowed him to conduct religious services for his parishioners in one of the halls at Kilruddery until the rage of the yeomanry had abated. Bishop Donnelly notes "this is a feature pleasing to recall and should not be forgotten to the noble family of Meath". Because of the priest's care of his flock during those appalling years the parishioners, in grateful appreciation, fenced off some acres of the commons on the lower slopes of the Sugarloaf and they built a humble cottage for his residence. For some years, subsequent to the rising, the yeomanry were quartered on the poor people in Bray which resulted in great poverty which in turn depleted the offerings that were required to maintain the little building off Bray's Main Street. The rent of the small structure was two pounds per year and when it fell into arrears they were evicted, the thatched roof was tumbled and Mass was not celebrated there again until 1809. The chapel yard was where the fancy paving now is at the front and the landlord built two houses on it leaving a passage of eight feet behind these where he erected some small cottages.

A few years later Father Callaghan's cabin, on the lower slopes of the Sugarloaf at Kilmacanogue, was badly damaged by fire and an appeal was made for money to enable the cottage to be rebuilt. It is interesting to note that many Protestants were the main contributors which indicates the respect and regard in which they held him. Among the names of the generous donors are the Earl of Meath, Lord Monck, Lord Howard, Henry Grattan, Sir S. Hutchinson and Lt. General Cockburn.

Father Callaghan commenced to build a new chapel in Kilmacanogue around 1820. The chapel that stood before that was a tiny, poor, low-roofed structure erected hastily and almost by stealth in the early 18th. century, beside the ruins of the very old church, surrounded by the old tombstones. The remains of these relics from our melancholy past can still be seen on the south side of the road right opposite to where the new church is. Father Callaghan died on the 17th November 1823 and it was his successor, Canon Roche, who completed it by adding the front and tower. Christopher Callaghan is buried beside the new church but his grave cannot be identified. His age at death is unknown but it is thought that he was around sixty five when he departed this life. Dr. Nicholas Donnelly stated in 1899 that he had in his possession a portrait of him and described it as "an amiable old gentleman, attired in the customary knee-breeches and body coat, and the old fashioned white neck-cloth, then worn by clergy and laity alike". The inscription at the back of the painting read "The Rev. Christopher Callaghan, parish priest of Kilmacanogue and Bray 36 years. Died 12 November, 1823. This portrait was bequeathed by Miss Elizabeth Mc Keon to Rev. Walter Canon Lee and the succeeding parish priests of Bray". (The whereabouts of this painting is not known, perhaps it has been destroyed.)

FATHER JAMES DOYLE

Immediately after Father Callaghan's death the Rev. James Doyle was appointed on the 25th November. He was educated in the then newly established college at Maynooth and was ordained in 1808. Before coming to Bray and Kilmacanogue he was parish priest of Avoca. On his arrival he decided to change the parochial residence to Bray which annoyed his parishioners in Kilmacanogue. There were two reasons why he decided to do this. The first was that he had nowhere to live in the former 'mother' parish because Father Callaghan had died intestate and the small cottage that he lived in with the little bit of land devolved to his family. (It was returned to the parish some years later after much dispute). The second reason was that Father Doyle recognised that Bray would grow and become more populated. Number 103 Main Street (now the offices of the Trustee Savings Bank) became his temporary residence for a number of years. He commenced to plan and build a larger 'chapel' which could accommodate the increasing number of parishioners. Dr. Donnelly described the event as "We were still in bondage, and had not yet acquired the courage to call our sacred edifices their proper name of 'churches'. The old structure was a very humble oratory of small, low dimensions, but a witness of hard times and it was thought well not to change the site but to construct the new building round the old one, and thus consecrate a spot well-watered by the tears and trials of our suffering forefathers."

The first stone was laid in 1824 and the building was a simple broad parallelogram with a gallery at one end and the altar flat against the wall at the other, similar in style to St. Peter's in Little Bray. It was of such significance and importance to the people that it was referred to as 'the Great New Chapel of Bray'. During the building Father Doyle found a use for the heaps of stones and piles of sand that lay around the church. Habitual topers and other minor transgressors were made to stand on them with the nature of their faults written on notices attached to their persons. (This is what has been 'handed down' to us but I find it hard to believe that the priest would be so cruel. Perhaps it was done in a humorous and joking fashion with the acquiescence of the culprits.)

Father Doyle didn't live to see the new church completed. He died in June 1826 after serving as PP for a short two years and seven months and was buried in the church the place being marked by a memorial on the floor. Before he went to God he initiated the idea of a permanent and comfortable residence for the Parish Priest of Kilmacanogue and Bray and purchased the site which to-day we know as St. Cronan's. The purchase of St. Cronan's was in his own name but before he died he made sure that it would pass to the church and made a will to that effect, no doubt in consequence of the memory of the difficulty which transpired from Father Callaghan's intestacy.

> *I, James Doyle, Parish Priest of Bray, being of sound mind bequeath half of my estate in the lease of Ballinacur, my late holding, to go to the support of my dear father and mother during their natural life, and other half to my nephew, John Doyle, provided he continue in his intention of becoming a clergyman, and in case my father and mother do not live to see the expiration of my interest in the lease of Ballinacur, then half of the said interest to be applied after their death to the purchase of moral and religious books for the adult and rising generations of Redcross and Rathdrum. Same to be done with the remaining half if John discontinues his vocation.*

> *The interest in my lands in Bray and vicinity I bequeath to Most Rev. Dr. Murray, to be disposed of as he may think proper, my books to be held over by Rev. A. Roche for my nephew, John Doyle, if not to Rev. A. Roche, Kilquade, for his life, afterwards to be disposed of in charitable uses. Twenty pounds to my sister, Anastatia Kelly. To Mrs. Mary Murray, otherwise Byrne, one suit of vestments with my chalice. All the residue I bequeath to my executors to dispose of as they may think fit. I appoint as my executors Rev. Alexander Roche, Parish Priest of Kilquade and Rev. John Grant, Parish Priest of Wicklow.*

CANON ALEXANDER ROCHE (ROACHE)

On 24th. of July 1826 Father Alexander Roche was appointed PP by Archbishop Murray. A nephew of Father Lowe, who was PP of Roundwood and Glendalough, he was born about 1784 near Rathdrum. He immediately commenced to build the parochial residence, St. Cronan's, which remained unaltered up to the arrival of Bishop Donnelly nearly seventy years later. The building to-day is much the same as it was then and it's now headquarters of the Bray Urban District Council who bought it from the parish.

In 1834 Archbishop Murray, in preparation for a visit to Bray, asked Father Roche to provide him with details about the parish and its churches. The information sent which indicated the poverty of the area at that time was:

> *Title of Parish - Bray, its dependencies, Kilmacanogue, Cuttlestown and Enniskerry. None of the chapels have been dedicated. Bray chapel held by lease. Rent, a peppercorn. Counterpart of lease deposited with Parish Priest. No lease of Kilmacanogue chapel, built on the Commons of Sugarloaf, no rent. Mass is celebrated in Enniskerry in an old barn belonging to a parishioner. Alas no ground can be found as yet to erect a new chapel. In Bray chapel, one chalice, one ciborium, five suits of vestments. In Kilmacanogue chapel, one chalice, four suits of vestments. In Cuttlestown, one chalice, one suit of vestments. In Enniskerry, one chalice, one suit of vestments. Five public Masses celebrated on each Sunday and Holyday in the parish, two in Bray and one each in the other three chapels.*

In 1853 the church was again enlarged and a belfry tower added in 1854. Father Roche died on the 31st. of July 1859 aged 75 and was buried in Kilmacanogue. There is a memorial inside on the wall of St. Canoc's marking the spot where his remains lie and the curious inscription states:

> *This monument was raised to his memory by friends who revered him living and deplored him dead.*

With the death of Canon Alexander Roche, Enniskerry and Kilmacanogue were made into a separate parish and Bray and Greystones became the responsibility of the new Parish Priest, Canon Miley.

CANON JAMES JOSEPH MILEY

A mong all the famous Parish Priests who have served in the church on our Main Street perhaps Canon John Joseph Miley might be considered the most remarkable.

The description of him in the Catholic Register, around 1844, when he was at the height of his fame read :

> *in stature he is tall and slight, with a clerical and commanding look; his countenance is of a pale, delicate and melancholy cast, with a meek and unruffled placidity which tells a mind at peace with all below, holding sweet converse with the spirits of a brighter world, and with such fervency do his thoughts sail from earth to heaven, that at times he looks like a robed statue, his very countenance wearing a calm, cold immobility of death ; but you have only to place him in the pulpit, and his frigid look evaporates neath the burning rays of his soul's devotion.*

He was chaplain to Daniel O'Connell and when the Liberator was imprisoned in 1844 it was Miley who was made regular visits to him in gaol. On O'Connell's release Miley accompanied him through Dublin in an open touring carriage where he was feted by countless thousands celebrating his freedom. Canon Miley was in London, in February 1847, when O'Connell made his last speech in the House of Commons, pleading for the end to the export of food from Ireland, when his health was failing fast. O'Connell wished to return to his suffering people within the week with Father Miley but his doctors advised him to go to the south of France to recuperate. They both decided to combine this with a pilgrimage to Rome. The travellers stayed for a while at Hastings on the Sussex coast in the south of England and the writer recently visited there in a vain attempt to find the inn or hotel where they rested. (One of the most likely had their visitors registers destroyed but still had preserved a list of important guests. Alas, this list were those with titles and no 'commoners' were considered worthy of inclusion. Another that might have helped in the quest turned out to have been the victim of a direct hit from a bomb in the 1939-1945 war and all that was found on the site was a small park in memory of those who perished within it.) When they reached Lyons, O'Connell became so weak that he was confined to bed and Father Miley noted "never had I had such a struggle as from two to four last night to keep him in bed, or to prevent the alarm being given to the whole hotel. It would have been most unfortunate that any but his own had seen him. Later on he wrote "by day I cannot leave him to walk in the

22

open for fifteen minutes and by night all his griefs and terrors are on me - for he will not be satisfied unless I am by his bed".

O'Connell made a slight recovery and they decided to chance going on to Rome but could proceed no further than Genoa. On Saturday, May 15th, as he lay on his death bed he asked those present to send his heart on to Rome and his body back to Ireland. His last words were addressed to the future Parish Priest of Bray "my dear friend I'm dying!" Father Miley completed the journey and brought the heart to Rome.

It was not until August that the Liberator's embalmed body was brought back to Ireland, a country filled with despair. As the ship, the Duchess of Kent, sailed up the Liffey with its sad cargo it passed another outward bound. The Birmingham filled with poor heartbroken emigrants fleeing from their barren fields forever. The sound of a loud wailing, lamentation and caoining rent the air as both ships passed one another.

The coffin was placed on a catafalque in the Pro Cathedral where it lay in state before the requiem Mass was celebrated. Father Miley preached the homily before a full congregation, comprised of all the principal dignitaries and prelates of Ireland, and then he accompanied the mortal remains of his friend to Glasnevin Cemetery.

Two years later saw Canon Miley as President of the Irish College in Paris, the first secular priest to hold this position and it was there that he remained for the next ten years. During this time he made a study of the Roman catacombs and the history of the Papacy which led him to publish a number of works on these subjects among which were Rome under Paganism and History of the Papal States. Paris was then the centre of the fashion world and he commenced the habit of possessing five wigs, the short one to be exchanged for the medium one, the medium for the long in accordance with what was thought the normal growth would be. In those days this was quite commonplace. He kept up this routine even when he was in Bray and would send the wigs back to Paris to be re-coiffured .

When he was in France he was befriended by Napoleon the Third who presented him with many works of art some of which he brought to Bray and presented to the church. As well as some valuable paintings, he presented the Stations of the Cross which are still there. The others were given to churches in the Bray area by succeeding parish priests of Holy Redeemer.

It was the famous Father James Healy, the head curate in the church at the time, who welcomed Canon Miley to his new parish. The parish priest of Bray and

Greystones had but a short time to care for his flock. He died on the 18th. of April 1861 and his body was buried in the church. Unlike Canon Doyle's remains, the place where he lies is unmarked but there is little doubt that it is where the old pulpit used to be.

In Memories of Father James Healy it is recorded: "Dr. Miley's health had been breaking for some months previous to his death. He brought away from France a wounded heart; but like the Spartan, he did not let those about him know how deeply it was gnawed."

The only will that Miley made was in 1837 and it reads:

> *pixis, oil-stocks, copy of Diocesan Statutes, and a purple stole (presented to him by Lady Ranelagh) to the Archbishop, Dr. Murray. To father, mother, brothers and sisters whatever article of my property they may select as a memorial, the article selected not to exceed £1 in value. Debts to be paid ; £5 to two orphans named Teigue, known to Williams*, £5 to Sisters of Charity for orphans recommended to them , residue, if any, to be applied one half for Masses for the repose of my soul, to be said in Marlboro Street, the other half to Sisters of Charity for sick poor of same Parish.*

One of the executors to the will was Father Burke who was PP of Saggard and Miley's papers were bequeathed to him. When Dean Lee succeeded Canon Miley he made enquiries from Father Burke about these documents and was informed "it was my custom, while making the assortment, to throw into the fire any letters that did not belong to the Cardinal." So that now not one scrap of Dr. Miley's writing in connection with the parochial administration of Bray survives.

DEAN WALTER LEE

Dean Lee was born in 1811 and entered Maynooth where he was ordained. In 1854 he left for Rome to continue his studies where he was conferred with a Doctorate in Divinity before returning to Ireland. Dr. Cullen, Archbishop of Dublin, appointed him PP of Bray on April 19th. 1861. He was responsible for the building of the church outside Greystones at Blacklion (one of the subscribers to this church was the Empress of Austria) and also for the Bray bell which still tolls for Masses, funerals and the Angelus. He presented the church with the marble baptismal font, which is now used for holy water, in the

* (A sacristan at the time - John Daly now occupies that position)

24

porch opposite to the Little Flower Hall. Dean Lee died on the 13th. of December 1893 and his obsequies were honoured with the presence of the Archbishop, two bishops, and a multitude of the clergy and his flock, whilst as a mark of respect from the non-Catholics of the parish, the Church of Ireland rector, Archdeacon Scott, had the great bell of Christ Church tolled during the funeral. He is buried in Glasnevin. In his will he left his silver gilt monstrance and ciborium to the church. A chalice was presented in his memory and it is used frequently, to-day, when Mass is celebrated.

It was rumoured that when he died he left vast wealth. In fact the amount he left came to £1,600 and, from this, his will stipulated that £1,000 be given to the college in Maynooth and £600 to the poor of Bray. Bishop Nicholas Donnelly had this to say of him:

> *Dean Lee has great claims upon your affectionate veneration. You all remember his courteous and dignified bearing as an Ecclesiastic, his affability and gentleness , his kindness towards the poor. No parish in Ireland was better organised than I found Bray when I came here near three years ago.We are bound then as a matter of common gratitude to perpetuate the memory of such a good man, and we are bound furthermore, as a matter of restitution, to give him back his good name so foully aspersed by those who too recklessly helped to circulate idle and calumnious rumours.*

Some time ago, whilst fruitlessly searching for documents which might help in research, many papers were found bearing Dean Lee's signature. There were none for any for the parish priests that preceded him and this, perhaps, proves his organisational ability.

DR. NICHOLAS DONNELLY

Dean Lee's successor was Bishop Nicholas Donnelly who was appointed by Archbishop Walsh on January 1st. 1894. He was Bishop of Canea, a town in Crete, and it was he who wrote the history of the Catholic Church in Bray as well as many Dublin parishes. Responsible for building most of the church that we see to-day, it was he who dedicated it to 'Our Most Holy Redeemer'.

The style of the old church from this time is late Romanesque with corbels and cornices in the Gothic fashion. The height to the cresting of the roof is 72 feet. The remains of the old altar rails are the work of James Pearse, father of Padraig. The Sacred Heart and Our Lady's altars are decorated with Sicilian coloured marbles and mosaics. The main altar contains panels of Venetian mosaic. Statues of the Sacred Heart and Our Lady were carved by a Mr. Smyth of Great Brunswick Street in Dublin and are created from marble. The massive pillars are of polished granite and are supported at the base by beautiful carved Portland stone. The sacristy was built at the same time, when it was completed Dr. Donnelly commissioned a Neapolitan artist, Eduardo Buccini, to paint three paintings, one of Leo X111, one of Archbishop Walsh and the third of himself holding the plans of the new church. These paintings, in their massive frames, still hang in the sacristy.

Well I think that I'd better leave Holy Redeemer for the moment, otherwise you'll think that this book is all about it. I'll return again later to muse about the Catholic Church in Bray but for the moment, recognising that the Protestant population is very much a part of our proud history, I'll dwell for a moment on the Church of Ireland.

CHRIST CHURCH (C.o.I)

Because of the great increase in the population from the middle of the nineteenth century, due to the coming of the railway in 1854, the very beautiful church of St. Paul's, (not to be so named until dedicated in 1869), was unable to accommodate the large numbers of the Established Church.

St. Paul's is the oldest of all the churches in the area that is not in ruins and its history can be traced back to 1609. It is believed that it was built on the site of an older church which, like so many others in our country, fell into decay around that time. There are ancient records, written in 1530, which refer to the Church of 'Bree' and this was called the Church of Derichat (a corruption of the old Irish word Dear-Teacht, meaning a house of penitence). More than likely this is the same site. A visit to the cemetery that surrounds it is recommended and you'll see many very old tombstones which have been well preserved because they're sheltered from the wind. The oldest legible one still standing is dated 1697 but without doubt there are many more ancient under its hallowed ground. Access to the cemetery is only possible on Monday to Friday through the gates on Church Terrace.

It was resolved to erect another church and Lord Herbert of Lea (the same person who gave his name to Herbert Road), who was also closely associated with the establishment of the National Gallery and Museum, and who also gave the ground for the old presbytery, now the Parish Centre in Most Holy Redeemer, granted a site on what was known as 'the Rock of Bray.' The Countess of Meath contributed the huge sum of £4,000 towards the cost and that was matched by a contribution from the Ecclesiastical Commission and the work soon commenced. (I dare say that you can multiply this by 100 to arrive at to-day's value). At the same time the Earl of Pembroke presented a site across the road and the rectory could also be built. It wasn't long before the shell of the church and the base of the tower was complete and on the 25th. of July, the feast of St. James, the building was consecrated by the Bishop of Killaloe in 1863. The tower was finished and the spire added in 1866 and the church was complete in all its majestic splendour. The architects were Carpenter and Sleator of London who designed it following the Gothic style, and it is constructed from Wicklow granite. The stonemasons were mostly local who took great pride in their work. Dimensions are 125 feet long and the tower rises to a dizzying height of 173 feet.

Over the following years many gifts in the form of furniture and memorials were added to finish the interior. The stained glass east window is in memory of the 10th Earl of Meath and the west one commemorates the 11th Earl. There is much carved wood mostly in walnut and this is the creation of the famous Bray Woodcarvers (I'll tell you more about them after this) who were closely associated with the church. The magnificent stained glass mosaic reredos dominates the altar. This is made up of Venetian glass and portrays the Transfiguration after a painting by Raphael. All around are carved figures of Irish saints and angels, frozen in time, offering silent prayer through the long years past and to come. The lovely little carving of Saint Patrick in the lectern is just one of many worthy of your close inspection. Inside the main entrance porch there is a Roll of Honour commemorating parishioners who were killed in the First World War and within there is a large brass memorial to the pupils of Aravon school who fell in that terrible conflict.

Lectern in Christ Church

When William Gladstone attended service here in 1877, while he was guest of Lord Powerscourt and visiting the Earl of Meath, he commented on the absence of bells in the tower and gave a donation of £50 towards a fund for their installation. The Brabazons outdid Gladstone by contributing £200 and it wasn't long before the bells pealed for the first time in 1881. They weigh a total of six tons and the largest is a ton and a half! They were all made in Loughborough, England.

Without doubt the most prominent figure to have been associated with the church was the Venerable Archdeacon James George Scott who had the distinction of being the last Vicar of Bray. The title 'Vicar' was abolished in Ireland when the Church of Ireland was disestablished in 1869. It is interesting that it was Gladstone who introduced the bill in the House of Commons to disestablish the Church, an event that was met with strong opposition as many thought that it was the first step towards the Repeal of the Act of Union. Archdeacon Scott had a long life, he died on the 12th of January 1912, and is buried in Delgany.

The Archdeacon's son, Canon George Digby Scott, succeeded his father as rector and it was he who wrote the greatest book on the history of Bray, The Stones of Bray. The granite Celtic cross that stands in front of the church is a memorial to both father and son and commemorates their service in Gaelic lettering.

Before proceeding further and introducing you to the lives of the famous and some ordinary people let me tell you, as promised, about the origin of the wood carvings inside the church. But first I'll dwell on the school called Aravon which I mentioned a few paragraphs previously.

ARAVON

Most people in Bray are familiar with all our wonderful schools, Bray School Project, St. Patrick's, St. Gerard's, St. Thomas's, Presentation College, St. Fergal's, Colaiste Raithin, Loreto, St. Peter's, Scoil Chualann, St. Andrew's, St. Killian's, St. Cronan's, Ravenswell and St. Brendan's but it is most surprising the number that are unaware of the existence of Aravon, which is one of our earliest educational establishments.

Its history commenced in 1862 when a Mr. Reginald Courtenay opened a small private school on Sidmonton Road and a short four years later it moved to the Meath Road to accommodate the rapidly increasing numbers of pupils. The name then was unpretentious, simply 'The Bray School' and it continued to flourish. When Mr. Courtney passed on, a Miss Haynes took charge of it around about 1873 and she remained there until 1892, during which time she was ably assisted by a number of headmasters, John Holdbrook, Mr. Mac Lean, De Burgh and Siddley when there were about 50 pupils in residence.

An interesting episode from this period was remembered by Mr. Frederick Eason, who at the ripe young age of 98, recalled that in the year 1876 a telephone was installed in the building. This came about because of the great friendship between their Mr. Holdbrook and Professor Bell, the inventor of the then amazing apparatus, who gave his friend a pair of receivers. The school, therefore, has the distinction of being the first establishment in Bray, and maybe in Ireland, to possess such an instrument.

When Miss Hynes retired a Mr. Cyril Smith managed the school for two short years until the arrival of Mr. R. H. Bookey in 1894. It was at this time that the name was changed to 'Aravon' ('Novara' spelt backwards, the buildings being on lands formerly attached to Novara House). Bookey was 55 years old when he arrived on the scene and he was to remain there until his retirement in 1924. Under Bookey's guidance the numbers of pupils increased greatly and its fame as one of Ireland's leading rugby schools was established as well as its reputation for academic distinction.

Bookey, in his early years, was a kind and considerate disciplinarian and was remembered by those he taught in those days with affection. As the years went by his manners changed and he became a person feared greatly because of the frequent and severe caning that he inflicted on the boys. It's thought that this change of personality might have been due to the fact that he became quite deaf and this in turn led to a sense of terrible frustration which he took out on his pupils.

Richard Hastings Bookey, as his name suggests, was totally upper class English and he continually stressed the admirable virtues that he believed were natural to that race at all times. Any other nationality was inferior and he always regarded the pupils as good little English gentlemen even if they came from Ireland, Scotland or Wales. This didn't go down too well with many of the boys who belonged to the Anglo Irish tradition and who were beginning to espouse the emerging spirit of Irish Nationalism. The school was as British as any public one in Britain, they celebrated the Queen's and King's birthdays, waved Union Jacks, stiff upper lip, eager to rally to the colours etc; but horrors of horrors, within the very bosom of that upper class institution there were some who, unknown to Bookey, harboured evil aspirations favouring Irish Republicanism – Tom Casement and his brother, the great Irish patriot Roger who was destined to be the sixteenth of the executed 1916 leaders, attended school there. The school's tradition was always very British and many of the children were sons of serving British officers. It is not surprising that during the First World War (the one that was to end them all) two hundred past pupils joined up. Casualties were high and forty two pupils and teachers were killed. In the Second World War one hundred and seventy joined and twenty four fell.

Famous rugby personalities of their time who had associations with Aravon were Dr. Robert Collis who was capped for Ireland, C.B. Nicholl who taught there was captain of the Welsh fifteen, H. Corley was capped eight times for Ireland, Poole Hickman who also taught there played on the Wanderers team that won the cup in 1906 (Corley was also on this winning side). Many of the masters and pupils were also distinguished cricketers.

In 1924 there was a disastrous fire in the school and most of the old records were destroyed. This greatly effected Bookey, his health quickly deteriorated, and was responsible for his long overdue retirement. He was succeeded by Arthur B. Craig, who was an old Aravonian, and he ran the illustrious institution for a long 28 years during which time the numbers of pupils continued to grow and many improvements and enlargements to the premises were carried out. Mr. Charles Mansfield joined Craig as Assistant Headmaster and eventually became Headmaster.

Mr. Cooper became Headmaster in 1970, and he introduced co-education, until 1973 when he became Principal when Mr. Roy Parker became Headmaster.The school badge and colours were designed by Bookey's wife; the ravens on the crest is a bit of 'heraldic' humour being a pun on the word A-ravon and the Latin motto translates as 'Our good name is our life'. Mr. Charles Mansfield's description of the school in the early 1970s was:

31

An atmosphere exists where Christian happiness, hard work, keen games and good food combine to develop all that is best in a child both physically and mentally.Aravon has kept the number of its pupils low so that the family atmosphere can be fostered, where every boy and girl is an individual and can be cared for according to his or her particular needs.

THE BRAY WOODCARVERS

If you attend services in Christ Church, Bray, whether you do so as a parishioner or whether you are participating in the many ecumenical gatherings that are held there, you would be excused if your thoughts strayed from prayer and became distracted by the great decoration and beautiful church furniture that surround you. Much of this is the work of the famous Bray Woodcarvers. This is a very small part of their story.

Their origins go back to the late 19th century, when mass production was in its infancy, when the artistic and creative work of human hands was so beautiful in its imperfection and so unique in so far as no two pieces were identical.

It all started with the choirboys. As a break from choir practice and as a part of their recreation, a Miss Kathleen Scott commenced to teach them woodcarving. Kathleen was the daughter of Archdeacon J. George Scott and her brother was Canon George Digby Scott.

The boys found this new craft extremely interesting and they produced many a small ornament which they proudly presented to their families and friends. As they grew older the articles created became more numerous and of greater artistic merit. The pupils, eventually, were no longer in the choir, they had grown up and progressed on to earning their daily bread and couldn't attend classes anymore, so Miss Scott commenced to teach them in the evenings. Shortly after another lady appeared on the scene who was to become the greatest influence on the school and on its future. Miss Sophia St. John Whitty was born in 1880 and when she came to teach in Bray she brought with her the knowledge that she had had learned in Bruges (Belgium), world famous through the centuries for its magnificent carvings. She was to become a member of the Council of the Arts and Crafts Society and the Guild of Irish Workers. She also studied at the Metropolitan School of Art in Dublin.

In 1899 the Agricultural and Technical Instruction (Ireland) Act was passed in the House of Commons and from it the establishment of the Bray Technical Instruction Committee. Miss Scott became honorary secretary of the arts section in the school and in 1902 Miss Whitty was appointed teacher of woodcarving.

So there they were, two refined ladies in charge of a class full of men. It was hardly surprising that, shortly after, the next logical sequence occurred, Miss Scott established a day class for ladies in October 1902. By December of that year there were sixteen senior advanced pupils enrolled and nine junior for evening classes as well as fourteen ladies for the day course. Shortly after Miss

Scott found that the ladies day class was difficult to administer under the rules and regulations of the Technical Instruction Committee and she requested that it be removed from the syllabus, that she be allowed to retain the fees paid by the pupils and that she continue with the class in a private capacity. This was acquiesced to by the Committee (amongst whom were Archdeacon Scott, Dr. Donnelly the bishop of Canea and PP of Holy Redeemer, Rev H. Glenn, Father Richard Colahan and J.W. Reigh of Bray Urban District Council). The work being produced became more numerous and more commercially valuable so that there was a deputation sent from Bray to the Department of Agriculture's offices in Dublin to propose a scheme to establish an industry in connection with the woodworking class.

Prie Dieu Christ Church
Photo by Geraldine Edge

On 4th November 1904 the following resolution was passed by the Committee: "Miss Whitty: The Committee recommends her appointment which is to be made by the Society or Company to be formed to carry on the proposed Furniture Industry, the scheme of which is to be submitted for the approval of this Committee and the Department of Agriculture. The Committee also are prepared to recommend the appointment of Mr. Colvin in connection with the proposed scheme. Note of thanks to Miss K. Scott proposed by Rev. R.F. Colahan seconded by Rev. H.P. Glenn concluded the proceedings."

Shortly afterwards the Bray Art Furniture Society Limited was founded and the Committee noted "that one half of the equipment necessary for the classes in wood carving and cabinet making be provided at the expense of the Committee on condition that the Industry supply the remainder - the Industry to have free use of entire. The Committee providing bandsaw, clamps and circular plane to cost respectively £10.15.0; £1.10.0 and £0.11.6, and the Industry providing lathe costing £16.0.0."

The work produced was exhibited far and wide and won many prizes at international exhibitions in Dublin, Cork and London. Miss Whitty was manageress and Miss Scott held the position of secretary and soon they developed a thriving business which they advertised as "Wood Carvers and Makers of Ecclesiastical and Domestic Furniture". They continued teaching and running the business up to the first world war when the hustle and bustle of life soon brought the Industry to an end. Part of their premises became a club for wounded soldiers who, as part of their rehabilitation, were taught some of the woodcarvers skill. Miss Sophia St. John Whitty died in 1926 aged only 46 and her remains were laid to rest in Enniskerry, but the beautiful things she created still live in some of the churches that surround us and serve as fitting memorials to her, more so than the greatest marble tombstones in some cemeteries. I sometimes wonder if the descendants of those who were associated with the industry in those days are still dwelling here in Bray. Here are a few of their names : James Colvin (Instructor), William Glover, Charles Scott, James Bellew (inlay specialist), P. Ring, J. Devane, Joseph Devitt, John Burke, Thomas Moore, Joseph Lynch, Walter Huston, Samuel Lee, P.Connolly, J. Malone, G. Magee, P. Comiskey, Sam Kirkham, James Lee, W. McCullagh and P. Murphy.

All associated with this industry were great artists and thinking of artists and their work calls to my mind another detail of Bray's contribution to Ireland's collection of wonderful paintings. Let me tell you about it.

THE ESTABLISHMENT OF THE NATIONAL GALLERY

It's surprising the great talent and numbers of good artists that dwell here and this is reflected in the local art galleries - The Hangman under the direction of Val Byrne (an architect) who is also an artist of note, The Signal down near the quaint and curious Albert Walk and the Craft on Main Street. Also each year there are many exhibitions held in other places around the town, The Heritage Centre and in many of the Parish Halls. Among our prominent resident artists were Gay O'Toole and his brother Tom, Paul Henry the great Irish landscape painter, Yan Goulet both sculptor and painter, who made Bray his home since he came here from Brittany after the last war, Mrs. Pat Murphy (whose husband, Paddy, is chairman of the Bray International Dance and Music Festival and is also responsible for mounting many art exhibitions in Bray) and Susie Fortune and many more. My musings on this subject reminds me of Bray's connection with the National Gallery and Museum in our capital city one and a half centuries ago.

In Bray we are familiar with the life of William Dargan (a Carlow man) and what he has done for us. We have paid homage to him by honouring his memory in recent years and we are inclined to forget how much more he contributed to the rest of our country; - for example, he built the great Victoria Channel in Belfast, and was one of the engineers that built the Holyhead railway before returning to Ireland where he was responsible for nearly every railway that was to be built from Dublin; and he was also the moving force behind the Exhibition of Art and Art Industry in Dublin in 1853. He made several fortunes and died, in 1867, penniless after investing all his money in schemes to improve Bray.

The Dublin exhibition was prompted by the one which was held in the Crystal Palace (long since burnt), London, and shortly afterwards a smaller one in Cork. It opened on May 12th and closed on October 31st 1853, during which period receipts at the door accounted for more than one million entrance charges (Queen Victoria visited the exhibition - she was allowed in free of charge and was so impressed that she visited Dargan at his home where she offered him a baronetcy which he declined to accept). Whilst the London exhibition concentrated on the industry of all nations the Dublin one went further and presented works of art borrowed from the continent as well as sources in Britain and Ireland. The great success of the event gave rise to the establishment of 'The Irish Institution' with the object of the promotion of art in Ireland by the formation of a permanent exhibition in Dublin and eventually of an Irish National Gallery. The Earl of Meath, from Kilruddery, chaired the first meeting on 1st. November 1853 and among the other committee members were Sir George Hudson of Hollybrook in Bray and William Dargan.

A short time before the formation of The Irish Institution a group of prominent statesmen and businessmen came together and set up The Dargan Committee whose object was to find "the best means of rendering a tribute of gratitude to our fellow countryman, William Dargan, for his unparalleled exertions, which, under the blessing of Almighty God have so singularly tended to benefit our country by developing her resources and directing the industry of her people". Lord Brabazon, Sir George Hudson and La Touche (with Delgany connections) were members of this group and their efforts quickly realised a sum of £5,000, a large sum then and sufficient to establish a fine memorial. The Dargan Committee eventually proposed the erection of a suitable building for the reception and exhibition of works for the fine arts and their applications to industry, to be called 'The Dargan Institute'. These ideals were so close to the objects of the Irish Institution that the Dargan Committee now offered their money to it.

Subsequent to many meetings and the most careful deliberation the site selected for the building was decided to be on Leinster Lawn, which was between Leinster House and Merrion Square, used then by the Royal Dublin Society. It was also decided that a national library and a public museum be incorporated into the plans. A special Act of Parliament had to be passed to make this possible. The Act was introduced as An Act to provide for the Establishment of a National Gallery of Paintings, Sculpture and Fine Arts, for the Care of a Public Library and the Erection of a Public Museum in Dublin. This Act was passed on 10th. August 1854. The library was intended to hold the volumes from Marshe's Library and the collection was to be transferred. The Board of Governors and Guardians of the library included Richard Whately, (Protestant) Archbishop of Dublin, whose son was Edward William Whately, Vicar of Bray from 1857 to 1862, and Thomas Lefroy who was Lord Chief Justice of the Queen's Bench and who lived in Bray.

Subsequent to many difficulties caused in trying to raise the large sum required for the now increased and more ambitious plans, the British Treasury eventually granted the necessary finance to complete the worthy project. The museum was opened on 31st August 1857 with a public lecture given by Dr. David Livingstone of the immortal words to be made famous by Stanley "Dr. Livingstone I presume?" The statue of William Dargan was placed outside the

National Gallery in December 1863 and the building was opened to the public on 30th January 1864 by the Lord Lieutenant and present were the Earl of Meath, Sir George Hodson, Archbishop Whately, Thomas Lefroy, members of the La Touche family and many others with Bray connections. Two other names associated with Bray were Breslin, who ran a large hotel in our town situated down where Katie Gallagher's (now owned by that prominent Bray Lion, Joe Duggan) now is, who was given the contract for catering at the Exhibition in 1853 and Sidney Herbert, 1st Baron of Lea (1810 - 1861) who originally owned the land on which the gallery stands. Many of the preliminary meetings to establish the museums, library and gallery were held in Herbert's Dublin residence at Upper Merrion Street. He is perhaps best-known to the people of Bray through his presenting the site for Christ Church on Church Road and by the naming of Herbert Road in his honour. Herbert Road was opened to provide a thoroughfare to his large estate which was between Enniskerry and Bray.

ST. ANDREW'S (Presbyterian)

The origins of this church, on the Quinsboro Road, go back to the beginning of the history of Presbyterianism in Ireland. When the plantation of the nine counties of Ulster occurred, early in the seventeenth century, it was mostly people from Scotland who came over and among them were large numbers of these dissenters. There was a further increase when General Munro landed with an army of ten thousand to put down the rising of 1641. Congregations were rapidly established in the north and gradually spread south during the latter half of the seventeenth and early eighteenth centuries.

In the early part of the nineteenth century there was a record of two congregations in Wicklow but these gradually ceased to exist until one in Bray was established, meeting for services in a small 'chapel' on Main Street. This, then, was the only congregation in the whole of County Wicklow.

Along came the awful Hunger and many once prosperous Irish and Anglo Irish landowners were left bankrupt resulting in them having to sell their land. A government body was set up under what was known as the Encumbered Estates Acts to purchase and dispose of the properties which in most cases were sold at very cheap prices. One such unfortunate landowner, a Mr. Jessop who was a member of the Established Church, occupied the Tinnapark estate, just south of Bray, and it was purchased by a John and Helen Clarke, from Scotland, in 1851. The demesne consisted of 300 acres of pasture as well as a large area of mature forest. The Clarkes had a thriving thread making business in their homeland and they soon commenced to fell the oak trees to make bobbins for their factory in Scotland. They brought over their own workers nearly all of whom were Presbyterians.

The nearest place of worship, Bray, was difficult to attend on a regular basis, so they established a little school and a mission building on the estate where they held services every two weeks - the minister coming from Bray to officiate. In between the services at Kilpedder they travelled to Bray. Bray's little church, shown on the Ordinance Survey Map of 1838, and situated on Main Street, became too small to accommodate the increased numbers so a new and larger building was opened on the Quinsboro Road in 1858, it was enlarged in 1890 and again in 1895 to serve a congregation of 300. Within there is a very pretty plain oak pulpit which was presented by Sir Stanley Cochrane (of mineral water fame). It was, perhaps, made by the Bray Woodcarvers.

Subsequent to this there was a further increase in their numbers living in Greystones, due to the coming of the railway, and they had to travel to Bray and

Kilpedder for services. Pressure on the minister in Bray became so arduous, with the three communities to look after, that eventually he was unable to attend Kilpedder on Sundays and instead conducted services there on a weekday in the afternoon. The school established by the Clarkes continued to grow and visiting ministers from Scotland, the nine counties of Ulster and Bray continued to hold services there. With the growing numbers it was decided to build a church in Greystones which would cater for the needs of those there and in Kilpedder. William La Touche presented them with a site and the new church was opened in 1887. The builder was Thomas Evans of Greystones whose family have had long associations with the Church of Ireland along with the Spurlings and they have had a prominent history with the Coastal Life Saving Service (I'll introduce you to these two families and this Service later on in this book).

At the time of the opening John Clarke had died and his wife Helen was in Scotland but her brother, William Davidson, who managed the Kilpedder farm, attended the ceremony. Helen returned shortly after to Ireland but left for good the following year when she returned to Scotland.

Services continued in Kilpedder until 1939 when the little wooden church was given to the Church of Ireland in Delgany and thereafter Church of Ireland services were held there every three months until 1968.

The first record of a Presbyterian minister, that I could find, is in 1849 when the Rev. James Patterson was there. The first appointed to Greystones and Kilpedder was the Rev. Samuel Lundie, a native of Cavan, in 1890 and a Rev. Clarke who was looking after the church on our Quinsboro Road.

Before leaving the history of St. Andrew's a few words about our Methodist Church is appropriate. The church was erected in 1863 when Rev. Samuel Dunlop was in charge but before that there was a lecture hall and manse (still standing) erected by the Rev. Adam Averell in 1797. Services were conducted in a room by the Rev. Thomas C. Maguire in 1845. The Rev. Samuel Larminie occupied it as a mission station in 1847

Permit me to now to go back again to the Catholic Church, this time St. Peter's which is the third oldest church in the town, St. Paul's (Church of Ireland and now an organ factory) and Holy Redeemer being the other two.

ST. PETER'S (R.C)

Although St. Peter's was built in 1837, before the coming of the railway, it didn't become a parish until Father James Healy was appointed in 1869. Its history goes back further because of the strange circumstances that led to its foundation.

The story starts in Dublin around about the year 1750 when a group of worshippers were attending Mass in a stable near Hawkins Street (where the old Theatre Royal used to be). There was a violent storm which caused an overhead chimney stack to fall through the flimsy roof and a number of the congregation were killed and injured. The tragedy was reported in the popular press at the time and many liberal Protestants were appalled to learn that some of their neighbours were compelled to pray in such squalor. The Royal Dublin Society was then situated close by and they were about to move to new premises near Leinster House so they donated part of their old site for the building of a small chapel, this was to be known as 'The Gentleman's Chapel'. Daniel O'Connell heard Mass there when he was in Dublin and later on he purchased a new site for a large substantial building in Westland Row, later to be called St. Andrew's, and the Gentleman's Chapel was closed. There was a beautiful reredos in the old chapel and it was carefully stored away.

Now let's come back to Bray. There is, on Old Connacht Avenue, the ruins of an old church surrounded by a cemetery which has been used up to modern times. This is where Mass was celebrated in the past but like the rest of the buildings it decayed and was in ruins around about 1630 having suffered the same fate as all the others. Nearly two centuries later it was decided to build another, this time at Crinken, which was convenient for the population of Shanganagh and Little Bray. The church was opened around about 1810 and stood on the Bray - Shankill Road, where the entrance now is to Shanganagh cemetery, on land belonging to a Mr. Mangan. There appears to have been a lot of trouble there, mostly on Sundays after Mass, perhaps due to the fact that there was a public house opposite to it. (I'm not suggesting that there's anything wrong about a pub near a church but in those days abuse of alcohol was a lot greater than to-day). Anyway faction fighting became quite common with crowds from Bray and Shankill going out to Crinken and thrashing one another until the landlord could no longer bear with the carry on so he requested the priest, Father Sullivan, to leave. He was quite polite and reasonable as it appears that he allowed them four years to find another site which they did in Little Bray on land belonging to a Mr. James Coghlan at

Gurchen's Lane. The only sign of anything belonging to the little church at Crinken is a large granite cross, quarried and carved in Glencree with the date 1810 at its base, which now stands in the old cemetery of St. Peter's.

The reredos from the old 'Gentleman's Chapel' were taken out of storage and placed in the church when it was completed and opened in 1837. The style of the interior can be described as neo-classical and an imitation of the architecture of the ruins of the destroyed city of Pompeii which had just then been discovered and which had become all the new fashion for churches. The floorboards in the sanctuary were lifted a few years ago and underneath were found two panels, belonging to the original reredos, decorated with floral and Eucharistic symbols.

The Stations of the Cross are by the famous Irish painter George Collie R.H.A and are most extraordinary as, unlike most others, they are bright and colourful. Inside the porch is a holy water font presented by Father James Healy's sister in memory of him. The magnificent painting above the tabernacle, the crucifixion, is thought to be of Spanish origin and many centuries old.

This was one of the first churches to be built in south Dublin and north Wicklow after Catholic Emancipation. Like all the others it was removed from the main road and the public house was in front of it as it is to-day.

The cemetery was opened in 1842 and enlarged again in 1905 and 1945. Many of the priests from the area are buried here, including Canon Piggot who has inscribed on his tombstone "see you later".

In the year 1843, a name on everyone's lips was Father Matthew whose fame had spread far and wide for the work he was doing for temperance in Ireland and Britain. A contemporary English newspaper described him as:

> One of the most remarkable men of our time, who has won for himself honourable fame, and a high place in the esteem of the wise and the good. He takes the place among the men who have been powerful in their day, for good or evil, by influence acquired over the minds of their fellow men, who have swayed the current of popular thought and feeling, who have effected revolutions in the habits, manners and opinions of nations. To inform the ignorant, to stimulate the backward, to bend the stubborn spirit, to purify the depraved heart - this is his province, this is his task.

And of the effects of his work on the people of Ireland they said

> Honour then to the 'Isle of Saints' as well as to the apostle of that popular movement which has awakened into fresh life and activity the

energies of her children, and set them free from the torpid lethargy of sloth and vice, which so long hung like an incubus on society, deforming its aspect, cramping its facilities and impending its operations. Should they have virtue and determination to persevere, Ireland will no longer be proverbial among the nations for squalid wretchedness; comfort and opulence will take the place of poverty.

Bray was soon to be honoured by the visit of this famous Cork priest. In 1845 Father Matthew preached here, in St. Peter's, and administered the pledge to 8,000 people.

Now, you're probably wondering how his homily managed to be heard by the multitude. After all he was speaking within a church which was built to accommodate a mere few hundred people and at that time there were no microphones or loudspeakers. The thousands were outside, those inside were tightly packed together overflowing through the porch, filling the yard outside and spilling into the Dublin road. Those within earshot would repeat the words spoken and those nearest to them would relay the phrases, and so on, until the people at the furthest edge of the crowd would get the message.

The church at that time is just as you find it to-day situated behind the Coach and Horses. Imagine the worry and despair of the poor landlord when he saw all his customers forsaking their stools and joining the multitude from all of Bray who were to reform and go 'on the wagon'. Picture the troubled brow of Mr. Watkins in the local brewery who was entertaining visions of his rapidly approaching destitution.

No report of his sermon survives but I can imagine what the content might have been. He would have described in great detail the poverty that results from overindulgence, the children and wives going hungry while the inebriated breadwinner is squandering the wherewithal in the nearest hostelry, the cruel and animal-like behaviour of the drunkard, the bloated visage, the red rimmed eyes, the purple nose, the loathsome stink and the early demise of the miserable wretch. He would have touched on the luxurious life style of the brewery owners, the foreign landlords and the overflowing coffers that the British exchequer get from the sale of drink in our miserable country (this would have appealed to the patriotic sentiments of his listeners). He described the strict judgement that God will mete out to the sinner and his burning in hellfire forever. The packed congregation groaned in their seats and the thousands outside beat their breasts murmuring mea culpa, mea culpa, mea maxima culpa!

Father Matthew was a great orator and his appearance was most striking. A contemporary description of him was:

> *His age is somewhat above fifty, but he looks younger; his frame is strong, evidently calculated to endure great fatigue, and his aspect is that of established health. He is somewhat above the middle size; his features are handsome as well as expressive. Our brief interview with him confirmed the favourable impression of his character we obtained from the knowledge of the benefits of his labours; and we left him with fervent thanks to God, that a man so qualified to sway the multitude had so wisely, so nobly, and so virtuously applied his powers and directed the energies of his marvellously active mind - feeling how dangerous he might have proved, if they had been exerted for evil and not for good.*

The Apostle of Temperance had gained such fame that he had, in Cork, his own brass band called 'Father Matthew's Own' which marched with him in all processions. At these processions and parades the crowds carried banners, on some of them there were portraits of him, others bore the inscription "5,600,000 regenerated sons of Erin" (this being the number that were reputed to have taken the pledge) and "All nations bless thee from afar, and hail thee Erin's radiant star".

The sincere and well intended promises of most of the multitude who took the pledge here, and in the rest of the country, was short-lived because of the appalling events that were to follow his visit in 1845. Famine, starvation and pestilence was to invade nearly every home and decimate whole communities. The poor people soon again took solace in the oblivion of drink to help them forget their dreadful but inevitable fate. We who are here in Bray to-day, because our forefathers survived the hunger, can see the living example of this great priest's work in the Pioneer Total Abstinence Association which has probably the highest number of members of any organisation in the world.

That's enough about churches for the moment and now I'll tell you about one of the famous persons who dwelt under of Bray Head.

WILLIAM CONYNGHAM PLUNKET

During a recent visit to Mount Jerome Cemetery, whilst I was researching the history of The Cripples Home*, I came across many tombs and monuments where the remains of famous people from Bray's past lie mostly forgotten and long faded into obscurity. My eyes strayed to the name William Conyngham Plunket and it struck a chord in the recess of my memory.

Born near Enniskillen in July 1764, he was the son of a Presbyterian minister who served there for twenty years before moving to Dublin when he was appointed to Strand Street chapel. William was the youngest in a family of three brothers and two sisters. He attended a school run by a Reverend Lewis Kerr for a short time until his father died. They had little means of support and young William, who was only fourteen, led a Spartan life for a few months until the congregation and friends came to his mother's assistance by collecting a large sum for her future support which left her in comfortable circumstances for the remainder of her life.

In 1779 William entered Trinity College, was a friend of Wolfe Tone who was a fellow student, and three years later he joined the Historical Society where he became renowned as an orator of outstanding ability. The Irish House of Commons was just across the road, in College Green (now the Bank of Ireland), and Plunket became a regular visitor to its galleries where he listened enthralled to the eloquence of Henry Grattan who made a great impression on him. Graduating with a B.A degree in 1784 he proceeded to London where he studied law and entered Lincoln's Inn. Life in London was lonely compared with Dublin at that time so he returned home in 1786 and was called to the Irish Bar in 1787.

From then onwards his career was meteorlike. The Provost of Trinity was accused of influencing a university election in favour of his son and Plunket became involved in the cause of his defence. The publicity from this, his eloquence and oratory, brought him to the immediate attention of those with great influence and soon he became one of the leading advocates in Dublin. In 1792 he married Catherine McCausland, daughter of an eminent Fermanagh solicitor, and five years later he received his silk and practised mostly in the equity courts.

In the cruel and terrible year of 1798 he was offered a seat in the Irish Parliament for the borough of Charlemount to which he was elected. He appeared to be a patriot and used his position and influence in the aftermath of

* This book has been published and is available from Sunbeam House, Bray.

the rising to plead for mercy and clemency towards the United Irishmen. He begged the Government to soften their acts of vengeance on his fellow countrymen and to cease the widespread tortures and executions.

Supporting Grattan in his opposition to the infamous Union, which was to abolish the Irish Parliament through the subterfuge and bribery of Castlereagh and Cornwallis, he made a memorable speech in the House in which he described the Union and his attitude to it. Some of the extracts are as follows:

> *It is a question whether Ireland shall cease to be free. He (Castlereagh) has exposed this project in it's naked hideousness and deformity. I say that if you ever mean to make a stand for the liberties of Ireland, now, and only now, is the moment for doing it during the administration of this unassuming stripling (Castlereagh). Within these last six weeks, a system of black corruption has been carried on within the walls of the Castle which would disgrace the annals of the worst period of the history of either country. I tell you that if you pass this Act it will be a nullity and that no man in Ireland will be bound to obey it. I am called on to surrender my birthright and my honour. For my own part, I will resist it to the last gasp of my existence and with the last drop of my blood and in the hour of death I shall not be haunted by the reflection of having basely sold or meanly abandoned the liberties of my native land. Can every man who gives his vote on the other side this night lay his hand upon his heart and make the same declaration ? I hope so. It will be well for his own peace. The indignation and abhorrence of his countrymen will not accompany him through life, and the curses of his children will not follow him to his grave.*

Such strong words but, alas, they meant little. Most politicians, just like to-day, enjoy the sound of their own voices and their principles and resolve can be overcome by material reward.

The Union was carried and Plunket submitted to it, notwithstanding all that he had said in opposition to it. During the state trials of 1803 he was involved as counsel for the Crown in the prosecution of Robert Emmet, which resulted in Emmet's cruel and barbarous execution subsequent to his persecution in Kilmainham Gaol under the control of the infamous Dr. Trevor. The vehemency and fierceness of his vitriolic abuse of poor Emmet, in the court, damaged his popularity in Ireland but brought him favour in London. After the trial he was appointed Solicitor General. Two years later he was elected MP for Midhurst (England) but a dissolution of parliament took place soon after and he didn't go forward for re-election until 1812. In the interim period he pursued his chosen profession and became the highest paid lawyer in Ireland. The accumulation of his wealth increased further with the death of his brother, Dr. Patrick Plunket, who left him a fortune of £60,000 (in to-day's values that's in excess of five million pounds!) In 1812 he entered the British Parliament as member for Trinity College. He was again appointed Attorney General in 1821 and kept this position until 1827 when he was appointed Master of the Rolls in England but resigned after a few days because the English Bar objected to an Irish lawyer being given such a high office. As compensation for his loss of office he was created Chief Justice of Common Pleas in Ireland and also made a peer under the title Baron Plunket of Newton (Cork). In 1830 he became Lord Chancellor of Ireland an office he held until 1841, when he resigned.

Baron William Conyngham Plunket spent the remainder of his life in Ireland at his home at Old Connaught in Little Bray. He died on the 4th. of January 1854 aged 90. His obituary reads:

> *With future generations his great and deserved reputation will rest upon a narrow foundation. His speeches were at once few and famous; they excited the unqualified applause of the age in which he flourished, while men who have survived these days feel that, even after a lapse of thirty years, his celebrity has scarcely waned, and that Plunket is still a conspicuous name amid the orators of the nineteenth century.*

Plunket's son, Rev. William Conyngham Plunket, was Vicar of Bray from 1825 to 1857 and his grandson was Archbishop of Dublin.

That's enough about famous people for a while. Let's take a look at the lives of the plain people of Bray in the mid-nineteenth century and we'll return to some of our prominent residents later.

THE PLAIN PEOPLE OF BRAY

When we talk or think about history, we remember the names and deeds of famous and sometimes infamous people because they are given the credit of having shaped the past. In Bray we eulogise William Dargan who is referred to as 'the father of modern Bray', John Quin who did as much for Bray (and maybe more) as Dargan, the Earls of Meath who gave us back some of our land and paid for the building of the town hall (McDonalds), Mr. Watkins who established the old brewery, the Powerscourts (Wingfields) who charge us to view the lands of the O'Tooles and O'Byrnes, Henry Grattan who lived near the town and many more. These people were news in their lifetimes. The chairpersons of the local council have their names inscribed in gold lettering on the boards in our Council Chamber and their signatures are enshrined forever on deeds and edicts that have come from their hands. The tombstones and stone memorials to the dead testify to their worth and the esteem in which they were held by the living. Were they as important as they were made out to be? If Dargan hadn't brought the railway to Bray surely another entrepreneur at the time would have. If William of Orange didn't defeat the Irish at the Boyne, Aughrim and Limerick, then James would have won and there would have been some of his supporters on the lands. If John Quin hadn't opened his small inn on the Main Street then, no doubt, another innkeeper would have. Breslin perhaps? Of course they were important but I doubt that they were as important as the 'little' people whose names we have forgotten. The giants of our history would not have survived without them but these 'plain people' would have survived without the giants.

In the course of my investigations and preparations for the setting down of a time capsule, to celebrate the bi-centenary of the foundation of the Catholic church on our Main Street, I was surprised by the scarcity of documents relating to the past. I had information on the various parish priests and important prelates who were associated with the building during its two hundred year history (see previous chapter); but details about the parishioners were scarce, which was surprising as one would imagine that letters and documents would be plentiful because of telecommunications not being in existence. It's true that the names of all the people are recorded in the parish records of baptisms and marriages going as far back as 1792 but there is nothing to give any indication of the feelings or thoughts of these 'little' people. I had all but given up searching. Despair at finding anything worthwhile had dampened my enthusiasm, especially when I learned that we had a parish priest who lit his pipe with spills made from all correspondence, when one day I noticed a tiny piece of paper sticking out of the panelling near the ceiling in the sacristy. With the permission and assistance of John Daly, the Sacristan, my search was soon coming to an end. The ceiling is about twelve feet in height but the problem of investigating was soon solved with the help of a ladder borrowed from Gerry Ryan, who was landlord of the Glenmalure Lounge at the time and who now plays about with a bulldozer. There was barely enough space for my hand to fit through the narrow aperture. Perhaps, I thought to myself, it's only one scrap of paper. I managed to extract it, and another followed by hundreds of black dust covered letters and documents dating from the period 1840 to 1897. Here was part of the missing history of Bray that told the forgotten story of the ordinary people who made the town. The people who toiled and sweated, laughed and cried, lived and died a long time ago. There is no memorial to them, let these scraps of paper serve to correct this.

It's not possible to do justice to them within these few pages there are so many of the documents but nevertheless I'll attempt to present a good cross section which will bring to light the goodness, the joy, the sadness, the hopes and the fears of these 'little' people. In all cases I've left out the names and addresses in order to respect the privacy of their descendants who might be living here to-day.

A sad and a brutal letter, but by no means the most melancholy in the collection, is a message from the Rathdown Union Master's Office in Loughlinstown which reads:

> *Madam, I have to inform you that your husband died this morning, please let me know by the bearer whether you will have his remains removed for interment.*

A letter from Van Diemen's Land, dated 25th June 1855, brings tragic news for a wife and son :

> *My Dear Mrs X., I write to you with the deepest regret and with great sorrow about the death of your husband. I am sure it must be sorrowful news to you and your child. God help you but God will be a father to you and your child. Dear Mrs. X. I may as well break the sad news to you. He was in Friars Creek jail he died. It is 30 miles from Melbourne. Don't be alarmed for it was for no crime and the police acted badly but if he was only in Old Ireland he would have been treated well. Tell Mrs. Q. William and I send our kind love to them and old enquiring friends. You would oblige me very much if you are going out to Dalkey tell Mrs. W. I have seen Maria in Melbourne. No more at present but still remain your well wishing friend, MS.*

Another letter, written from New Zealand and dated 1864, informs a widow that her husband also died in gaol and that he had the priest before he went to God and the letter goes on to say:

> If you take my advice you will come out to Australia. Their is any money here for good servants. Don't fret you are able to earn your bread anywhere you go. This is six letters I wrote to you and never got an answer. Dear G. I hope this will reach you and if so send me word that you and all my friends are well. I like this but not as well as Ireland. H. has very good wages but everything is triple the price here. If they would work at home as they do here they would have Australia at home in place of here.

Quite a number of documents relate to applications for permission to marry. One of the most beautiful is addressed to the parish priest and dated 1864, just nine years after the railway came to Bray and states:

> Dear Dr. Lee, it's but a scant biography I can give you of TKO, I never knowingly saw him but once, and was then sick a bed, he has been resident here during the past six months, I am sorry he's got a check in his progress to the Altar of Hymen, but old ways are changed, old manners gone, the path to matrimony formerly was bland and pleasant enough but now the way to it is thorny and rugged and beset with barricades, it's hard for an old fellow to chime in with the new ways and new fashions of these rapid railway times, but as the natural state of society is progress we must conform to them.

And this from a mother in respect of her daughter (written by a curate in the mother's parish because she couldn't write):

> ...your mother gives you cheerfully what she could not refuse in reason- her consent, but remembers something about past money favours which she fears she will not receive in the future. She would hope your future husband may be brother of the Chairman of the Bray Town Commissioners and then would expect no end to P.O money orders.

Now here's a message from an irate father. I can't help wondering what his son did that could prompt such a reply:

> The most rev'd. You have wished to see me. I have something else to do besides going to look after a useless mission of that sort. If your reverend is pleased to make the best hand you can of him as he has been of no use to me. No more at present.

Bray's connection with the American civil war is noted in documents referring to men serving on Confederate privateers. One of these papers gives the address as 'The Confederate Steam Ship - Georgia' and is dated 1864. Another states " M.D, three years on a confederate privateer and spent seven years in Little Bray and is going to join the Rapahannock on Tuesday". As well as these there are papers signed by Cardinal Paul Cullen and the Archbishops of Dublin at the time. Also letters from the British Admiralty and army, one such example reads:

> *Clonmel, Friday. I write to let you know that I will be in Dublin on Monday. I can't say what time but I will send you a telegram when I am starting so as you will know what time the train will be due at the Kingsbridge and if you can meet me do so. I could not come on Saturday as I have to leave all my harness clean for inspection on Monday morning. It is not easy to get leave as you think but the Battery will be in Dublin for a month for the practice for the review. Saying quite enough as I hope with the help of God to soon see you. Yours P.*

Other documents give us little bits of history, perhaps trivial, but someday they will be important. For example, the organ broke down and the letter from the parish priest to the organ builder reads "some pedal pipes do not speak and the keyboard requires regulating". The organ builder, a Mr. T. White, has on his stationery "T. White has Testimonials from some of the most distinguished Ecclesiastics and Musical Professors to whom he can refer with confidence" and he wrote back to the PP: "I will commence with the cleaning, repairing and tuning of your organ on Monday 9th of March according to agreement to complete same within two weeks to satisfaction for the sum of seven pounds ten shillings".

Most of the papers found contain details of everyday parish life and the names written are those that are prevalent in our town to-day. I list them at random: Dodd, O'Toole, McKeon, Doyle, Tobin, Byrne, Kinsella, Forde, Fortune, Murphy, Sutton, Daly, Devitt, Bowden, Humphries, Mc Garry and many more. These were the real makers of our history and are the true founders of modern Bray.

MR. QUIN'S HOTEL (The Royal)

Mr. John Quin - that's correct, only one 'n', established his inn in 1776 where Jim Mc Gettigan's Royal Hotel stands to-day. It was from the outset a busy place where weary travellers were refreshed on their way between Dublin and places further south. The coaches stopped here and the ladies and gentlemen alighted in anticipation of tasting the culinary delights for which the famous premises soon gained a reputation for. As well as those en route to other destinations, Bray's surrounding countryside, soon to be renowned for its beauty, attracted tourists who made the inn their base for daily excursions. The wonder of the waterfall at Powerscourt, the spectacular woodlands in the Glen of the Downs, the towering grandeur of Bray Head with it's Cambrian rocks sloping into the sea, the Sugarloaf and the pleasant walks along the banks of the Dargle, enticed visitors not just from Dublin but from all of Ireland, Britain and the continent.

Quin was an entrepreneur well in advance of his time. He recognised the potential rewards to be gained from tourism and developed his property accordingly by enlarging his inn and purchasing more land which he landscaped for the benefit of his patrons who were to spend many pleasant hours walking through his gardens down to the estuary where the river meets the sea. In the early years Henry Grattan was a regular visitor to the hotel and Daniel O'Connell was wined and dined within its rooms.

Many fashionable balls were held there, attended by the nobility and the officers from the surrounding garrisons, with the music being played by local military bands. The then modern works composed by the Strauss family, the glittering of a hundred candles magnified and reflected a thousand times by the numerous chandeliers, charmed the assembled ladies and their escorts as they swung around and around to the strains of the waltzes and mazurkas.

The 1850s was to bring the engineering pioneer, William Dargan, to Bray (as well as Isambard Kingdom Brunel) and he like all the others was to follow their example by partaking in the hospitality offered by the hotel. Dargan became a close associate of Quin and they were both responsible for providing the finance for the building of many of the early Victorian houses in the town.

Every important visitor recognised and enjoyed the food and comfort provided by the establishment and its fame spread far and wide. Thackery, the great traveller and writer, in his Irish Sketchbook written in 1842 and published in 1843, states:

at Bray is one of the best inns in Ireland; and there you may be perfectly sure is a good dinner ready, five minutes after the honest car-boy, with innumerable huroos and smacks of his whip, has brought up his passengers to the door with a gallop.

It was in 1852 that Mr. Quin opened up a public road to the sea and that's how Quinsboro Road obtained it's name. Around the same time the hotel was enlarged just in time for Mr. David Edge to build a new and wider bridge over the river in 1856. This was the third bridge to be built there and despite numerous floods with roaring torrents of water crashing down to the sea it still stands. In the course of construction Edge dined in the hotel. With all this

Bray Bridge

progress John Quin became more active in the affairs of the town and when the boundaries were extended in 1866 he became Vice Chairman of the new town commission.

The proximity of the courthouse, opened in 1841, provided 'mine host' with further custom and on days when the court was in session the hotel was filled with all those involved in the administration of justice and the Maltings, the brewery just across the road, helped swell the numbers partaking in the liquid nourishment available within. The thriving and most popular hotel was described by another celebrated writer, Gaskin, in 1869 who wrote:

Mr. J. Quin may be justly styled the 'father of Bray'. His hotel has a European reputation. He lived many years to enjoy the affectionate intercourse of his numerous friends. 'Quin, of Bray' had a kindness of heart which made every tourist who visited Wicklow his well wisher.

Specialities of the a la carte menu at the time were fresh Dargle salmon, sea trout, lobster and a large variety of fish caught on the same day off Bray Head, Wicklow venison and the usual assortment of other meats which were cooked on spits over open fires in the large dining rooms. Pheasant, partridge and snipe appeared on the bill of fare when in season.

Around about this time, the 1860s, hotels were springing up all over the place, the greatest competitor for John Quin being the International built in 1862 and having one hundred bedrooms. This large hotel never really provided the same luxurious atmosphere and personal attention for which Quin's establishment (now the Royal) was renowned. And what about the cost of all this comfort for the select fortunate and discerning patrons who could afford it? Six shillings, now thirty pence, was the price of a day's stay and this included a night's repose on a down filled mattress, a hearty breakfast, luncheon, afternoon tea and a sumptuous repast for dinner in the evening. The famous Shelbourne, in Dublin, at the time, charged six shillings and eight pence, now thirty four pence. This was above and beyond the wildest dreams of many of the poor miserable and wretched souls who inhabited our rapidly expanding town then.

It was business as usual during the War of Independence even though the police barracks was beside the hotel. The barracks eventually housed about forty men half of whose numbers were the infamous Black and Tans. As a small matter of interest I was once told by an elderly man, long gone to God, that Bray was the only town in Ireland where the 'Tans' were given cups of 'tay' and indeed it is a fact that the boy scouts from here went into Dun laoghaire to welcome the troops coming in to put down the 1916 rising! There was the occasional bit of sniping at night, evidence of which used to be seen on Dr. Thompson's memorial in front of the building but now, alas, the council have placed a new top on it thereby wiping out a piece of our history. This annoyance was not sufficient to disturb the guests in their beds. It would appear from the lack of casualties that both sides were rotten shots. The British Army took over the hotel in April 1921, a bad year for tourism! About forty years ago when the Church of Holy Redeemer was being reconstructed many straw mattresses and spent cartridge cases were found under its high roof and it is believed that the Volunteers probably slept there without the knowledge of either the priests or the sacristan. The army or the police never knew where the sniping was coming from but supposed it was from the grounds of St. Paul's, even though they never found any shell cases to indicate this. In fact the Volunteers were shooting from a safer distance, as far away as Ravenswell. Also about the same time, when the hotel was being renovated, a dumb waiter was found within the thick walls connecting the hotel with the barracks, indicating that refreshments were available for the Crown forces without their having to leave the building.

The hotel that you see to-day bears little resemblance to that which stood there at the end of the eighteenth or the nineteenth century. But within there remain some rooms and walls that are the same. Perhaps while you are sitting there in comfort you might listen intently and maybe you might hear a faint echo, the strains of 'The Blue Danube' and the far away sound of a military band reaching your ears from the distant past.

The Royal Hotel has a sister establishment down at the sea front, The Esplanade which shares the same luxury and comfort and which is becoming just as popular. John O'Connor and his lovely wife, Maureen (Jim McGettigan's daughter), together manage the hotels with a courteous and caring staff.

The sea front, Bray's greatest asset. Next I'll tell you a little about it.

OH, I DO LIKE TO BE BESIDE THE SEASIDE

Holidays! Well nowadays we're used to " having a great time wish you were here" in the Canaries, France, Spain, Barbados, Greece and other far away and exotic places. People in Ireland are travelling further and further in search of something different. Nearly one hundred years ago something different, the 'IN-PLACE', was Bray!

Yes indeed it was one of the great 'watering places', known far and wide as a great tourist attraction and its ability to cater for the large numbers of people who could afford to take a holiday. They came in their droves from all over, even from Dublin, with their cases and trunks packed and ready for a prolonged stay. Some of the very wealthy owned holiday homes here, just as today some

Bray Seaside

own places in the West of Ireland and some in Spain; others rented houses for a month but most stayed in hotels and boarding houses, where they were well looked after. Tourism was Bray's principal industry, as I believe it still is now.

What were the great hotels? I've already told you about the Royal which by this time was owned by a Mr. Arthur Odell. The International was owned by a Frank Bethel who also owned the Bray Head which had sixty rooms and the

Marine Station Hotel, on the site where Joe Duggan's Katie Gallagher's is now. These were the great and fashionable places to stay, where the cost was around seven shillings and six pence (now thirty seven pence) a day, which included your meals. Then there were the private or family hotels like the Holyrood on the Esplanade where the rates were from two guineas a week (a bath cost an extra six pence!). There was the Wavecrest run by Mrs. Harper who boasted of its 'London style attraction'. Mrs Mills ran the Esplanade, already mentioned, and it catered for vegetarians. Lacy's Hotel was also there then and a Miss Hurst took care of The Strand Hotel where your host is now Sean Fitzsimons, the Bray Lions used to meet there twice a month under the presidency of Lion Michael O'Brien, an eminent solicitor. In those days we were part of the British Empire and so it was not surprising that there was, as there was in nearly every town and city, a place called The Imperial which was situated in Goldsmith's Terrace on the Quinsboro Road. Of course we had, like every other small fishing place, a Harbour View Hotel and there it was at number 1, Seapoint, run by Mrs. Kenna.

All of these buildings were bulging at the seams during the high season; therefore it was necessary that further beds be provided and so we had one hundred and forty private houses offering board and lodgings from as little as ten shillings to as much as one pound a week, described as 'select private apartments, strict cleanliness, good cooking and attendance'. Every day the promenade and esplanade was filled with families and at mealtimes it was empty as they returned to where they were staying, where they dined at fixed hours. Most places served breakfast at 9, lunch at 1.15 p.m., afternoon tea at 4.30 and dinner at 7. The hustle and bustle as the crowd scurried to and fro, fearing that they'd be late for a meal that they'd already paid for anyway, presented a great and entertaining spectacle for the local inhabitants.

Of course all this also provided the shopkeepers with great profit, vast quantities of food consumed, souvenirs were purchased, presents for those less fortunate beings who were left at home, buckets and spades for children, hire of deck chairs, hire of boxes for those who wished to modestly undress, bathing costumes which practically covered the entire body, numerous boats for hire, regattas at Naylor's Cove and the licensed establishments selling alcoholic beverages. A description of the town for the intending visitor stated:

> *Bray provided a rich fund of Entertainment, Sport, Pastime and every variety of holiday pursuit, so that visitors to ' The Brighton of Ireland' need never be bored by lack of incident or bewail a moment's ennui.*

Coastguard Station

The town council had set up an Amusement Committee who were provided with what was then an immense budget of £800 which enabled them to provide military bands and concerts EVERY DAY on the promenade. There were fireworks, military tattoos and fetes, not to mention the magnificent display of turn of the century fashion as the wealthy paraded on the sea front. The railway station was a continuous hive of activity with its buffet, bar and numerous attendants and porters, jarvies and boots from the great hotels awaiting visitors. There were no less than one hundred and twenty trains a day, run by the Dublin and South Eastern Railway, in and out of the station. Even before the railway arrived Bray was a well known beauty spot. John Mitchel, as the ship on which he was being transported on passed the coast, wrote:

> *Dublin city, with its bay and pleasant villas - city of bellowing slaves-*
> *villas of genteel dastards - lies now behind us, and the sun has set*
> *behind the blue peaks of Wicklow, as we steam past Bray Head, where*
> *the Vale of Shanganagh, sloping softly from the Golden Spears, sends*
> *its bright river to the sea.*

The medical profession helped make Bray a popular resort for invalids. Surgeon Colonel Edgar Flinn, Medical Inspector of the Irish Local Government Board wrote:

> *Bray possesses unusual attractions, and has grown rapidly into*
> *popularity as a marine health resort of the first order. It is one of the*

most bracing of our seaside places, and is naturally in great favour with the residents of the Metropolis. The air at Bray is bracing and invigorating, and is especially suited to that class of cases where there is debility and general loss of tone, induced by overwork or long illness or other depressing agencies.

One hundred years ago a parish notice contributed to tourism by publicising this description:

Bray for the nonce has become a Dublin 'super mare'. The crowded appearance of the main thoroughfares, during the shopping hours especially, the gay aspect of the Esplanade all day long, with its Military Bands, its troop of minstrels, its multitude of happy children, and brightly attired children of larger growth; the air, the sea, the sun, the scenery, all combine to give a fairy semblance to the place, and render it one of the most delightful summer resorts for the tired-out business or professional man of family. This year Bray seems more crowded than usual. The unbroken fine and warm weather of May and June drove the city mice out rather earlier, and late comers found it difficult to suit themselves in apartments. To all we extend a hearty welcome, and venture to hope that all may derive great benefit from the sojourn amongst us, and return to their winter hive refreshed and re-invigorated.

Seafront and Bray Head

59

And a French lady, Madame de Bovet, had this to say:

> *Bray is entirely composed of hotels and bathing pavilions, clustering at the foot of a promontory of granite, which resembles a gigantic and good-tempered elephant, who shelters under his huge body the 'parade', a long jetty which runs the length of the beach. It is a pleasant sight. It is Dublin's 'Vanity Fair'. The women display their light dresses there, - white linen frock with saffron or orange sash, cinnamon coloured jacket, sailor hat with broad striped ribbon, black stockings and tan shoes, or else a dress of thin muslin or flowery chintz, with a fur cape on their shoulders. The daughters of Erin are naturally pretty. They are distinguished from their English sisters chiefly by their free-and-easy manner, which is very anti-English. The children are delightful- made up of strawberries and cream, with large blue eyes like forget-me-nots, or like velvet, and masses of frizzy hair, fair or dark; bare legged, strong, healthy and fresh as a dewdrop, lively and daring.*

Now wouldn't it be difficult for Bray Tourism to do better than that even with the outstanding talents and energy of Dermot de Barra who is presently doing a great job promoting our town! The population during the peak season rose by nearly thirty percent and this was most noticeable especially on Sundays when the bells of the churches rang out summoning the population, visitors and townspeople, to prayer and the pews were filled to capacity during all the services with standing room only and an overflow out and around the doors and porches, while they all listened to the homilies preached by Archdeacon Scott and Dr. Donnelly. Perhaps one of the great changes that have occurred here since that time is in the form of dress (or perhaps undress) that the warm weather and sunshine has manifested. Keeping cool has been the prime concern of everyone resulting in the most amazing sights on Main Street and on the Promenade. The once formal bank official or business man in a lounge suit has been transformed into a hairy legged, knobbly kneed apparition with bright Bermuda shorts and tee shirt and can no longer be distinguished from his humblest fellow at the lowest end of the social scale. And the ladies? Well now, they're very, very different too. The lightest and airiest of clothes that the fine summer weather has given rise to displays of fair skin, bare flesh and delicate feminine curves that a few decades ago would have been described as 'an occasion of sin'. What did they wear in those summers, long, long ago? Let's go back about one and a half centuries and take a brief look.

The average lady, because of financial restrictions, couldn't dress in what was fashionable. She wore what her grandmother had before her, a long dark heavy woollen frock or skirt which reached the ground and a few linen blouses perhaps with the great luxury of a lace collar and maybe some pretty floral embroidery. This was her wardrobe and I'm sure she looked very beautiful. Then there were those ladies who never engaged in the washing of clothes or the scrubbing of floors; Who never had to cook or carry a pail of water from a stream or a pump; Who never wanted for any material thing. Regularly they were seen in Bray entering and leaving Mr. Quin's establishment, decked out in all their finery like peacocks (peahens?). They were ladies of fashion and always dressed in the very latest trends that were all the rage in London and Paris. Vocabulary and turn of phrase was also fashionable being that of haute couture where French was added to English to impress their lesser informed listeners. The high fashions of those summers long ago were : Dresses of 'gazes de soie' in large shaded and striped patterns, made with flounces and headed by 'quillings' of ribbon. The taffetas had broad green stripes, separated by threads of violet, pink and gold and were trimmed with large plaits of ribbon in pink, violet and yellow satin, placed 'enechelle' up the front with bows of the same. Material made from 'poil de chevre' (goats hair) was in vogue for promenade costume and was made up 'en redingote', embroidered in round spots, and 'Brandebourgs' with flounces. 'Grenadines' (light dresses) with horizontal stripes of lilac and white were trimmed with five rows of fringed ribbon on the skirt and the body trimmed in like manner. The sleeves were long and tight, opening in the bend of the arm up to the elbow and fastened at intervals by lilac

Seafront

61

silk buttons, over half sleeves of white tulle, trimmed at wrist with lace. And there were the bonnets. For a lady of high standing to venture into public without a bonnet was absolutely a shocking spectacle, perhaps like a poor Bray lady attending church, in those days, without a scarf or shawl covering her head. The most fashionable bonnets were those trimmed in lace or 'gimp' (twisted cord or silk) lined with satin or those in lace and ribbon. The cost of one of these bonnets was about fourteen shillings which represented nearly twenty day's wages for the average working person.

All this finery still left something lacking - the parasol. It was then an object of great fashion and used to keep the fair skin from being blemished by the sun's damaging rays. An advertisement for one fashion shop selling them reads "W. & J. Sangster beg to submit to the nobility and gentry an entirely new parasol for this season. It will be sold retail lined and fringed at 10s 6d each or unlined at 6s 6d each. W & J.S also solicit an inspection of their extensive stock of fancy silk parasols suitable for the carriage, promenade, garden or seaside". And here we are, one and a half centuries later, lying out in the sun getting a tan so that we'll look good now and ignoring the fact that if we continue our skin will become, long before its time, wrinkled and dry like a prune.

While I'm on the subject of the sea front let me tell you about another famous building that's there.

THE MARTELLO TOWERS

On most Saturday afternoons I usually wend my way to the Harbour Bar where meeting my friends has become a ritual. Just a short way from my objective I pass the Carlisle Grounds which is the home of the local soccer team, Bray Wanderers, and immediately behind, on the seaward side is a large Martello tower.

These towers get their name from a corruption of 'Gulfe de Mortoli' which through usage became 'Martella'. This gulf is situated on the island of Corsica and in 1794 the British under the command of Lord Hood and General Dundas attempted to take the island from the French. The landing of invading troops

Martello Tower

was difficult because of the strategic position of a tower which overlooked the bay. The senior officer in charge of the British ships was Commodore Linzee and he landed his force on the evening of February 7th. to find that their advance was not possible because of the tower. The invading troops occupied a height that commanded the small fortress and notwithstanding a concentrated attack on it they couldn't manage to dislodge their French foes. Two of the warships, Fortitude and Juno anchored in the bay, fired a continuous cannonade at the tower for nearly three hours which appeared to have little effect. The firing from the tower at the ships was devastating and they were forced to weigh anchor and retire from the fray. The Fortitude was very badly damaged and both vessels suffered great loss of life. The French armament consisted of only eighteen pounders with which they fired red hot shot at their enemy. The attacking forces on the land continued to besiege and bombard the small fort for two full days until its garrison finally surrendered. Much to the surprise of the British they found that they had won a Pyrrhic victory, the French casualties being only two dead out of a total garrison of thirty two defenders. Inspection of the building revealed its hidden defences.

Constructed of granite, the walls were five feet thick which rendered them bombproof. The entrance was seven feet from the ground and admission could only be gained with the help of a ladder which was drawn within by the defenders. The parapet consisted of an interior lining of rush matting and was filled with sand. There were loopholes in the walls at an elevation that required the men to stand on benches when firing their muskets and these benches also served as their bunks. On the floor there was a trap-door which led down to a well equipped stores and ammunition room. The second floor entrance was also gained by means of a similar method.

The three Martello Towers, built in Bray in 1804 or 1805, were modelled on the one in Corsica as were all the others on our east coast and those on the shores of Britain, in Kent. They were built in order to repulse and warn of any French invasion. Fear of Napoleon was at its height and some sources at the time even referred to him as the Anti-Christ.

Number one tower was situated about a quarter mile north of Bray Head and was demolished when the promenade was being built. Number three was constructed a half a mile north of the Dargle estuary and it was destroyed by coastal erosion. The third tower, number two and the most important of the three, was built on high ground where it overlooked the whole area of the sea and the north and south beaches. This tower was heavily fortified and had many heavy cannon not just to defend it but also to inflict heavy casualties on any invading force. Because of its great size there was always a large garrison manning it. The garrison consisted of members of the '40th regiment of Foot', commanded by General Fisher who was responsible for all such fortifications in Ireland, who were also stationed at the tower in Sandycove and probably who gave their name to the bathing place nearby. Some people nowadays believe that the area was once called the Forty Foot because of the width of the area or the height of the tower.

This last tower is still there and was once inhabited by Bono of U2 fame. It's still an attractive private residence. While I pondered on the choice made for this last tower and its assumed impregnable position, my eyes wandered to what is without doubt the most unassailable site in Bray, and which occupies a view which overlooks the whole coastline, Bray Head.

THE CROSS

1950 was not long ago for many of us who can still remember it and who have now grown old. Most of the memories are happy ones and the one that stands out in that year is now a prominent landmark. The Pope had declared A Holy Year and here in Bray we were marking the occasion with extra ceremonies in the Catholic churches. All very spiritual but something material was lacking. It was Christy Dodd who approached Wally Byrne and asked him what special thing they were going to do to mark the occasion. They pondered long and hard. The parish priest at the time was Canon Moriarty, an exact image of what in Ireland was known as a 'Sagart Aroon', kind, old and everything that a venerable priest conjured up in the mind's eye. He would have reminded you of the parts in the old films played by Barry Fitzgerald the old Abbey actor. Anyway the old canon came from Wicklow town (his parish before Holy Redeemer was Castledermot) and as a student in Clonliffe College he used to cycle all the way home at some weekends to visit his parents. There was no public transport then except for the trains and money was always scarce. The journey was difficult - there were no gears on those 'upstairs' models then and it was exhaustingly strenuous pushing the pedals up so many hills. He told this to Wally on many occasions and said that, when he reached Shankill, he would look and pause at the wonderful sight of Bray's towering head and think that his journey would soon be over, even though he had many more miles to go. When he looked at the sight, he pondered thinking that it would make a wonderful place for a cross and he often mentioned this to Wally. Christy and Wally made the obvious decision and commenced their plans.

Father William (Liam) Breen, curate, made the application to the Council to build on the site and he submitted the plans for their approval. The Earl of Meath allowed them to transport the materials required through his land. Local engineer Fergus Clarke was responsible for all the technical work and remarked "I'll make sure that the structure stands firm for centuries!" Everything was ready for Sunday the 10th. of September and it was a glorious day but the plans were postponed because Wally was on his honeymoon with Monica and Canon Moriarty wouldn't proceed without him. So they all waited until Sunday the 17th. The weather was appalling, cold, wet, windy and most unpleasant but nevertheless they went ahead (no pun intended!). Wally was in the transport business and he brought up the sand, water, cement, scaffolding, tools, reinforcing steel and all else that was required on one of his three Bedford lorries. Francy Dodd was the foreman and he supervised the digging down to bedrock. They mixed the concrete in the mixer that Wally had brought along and poured it into the hole but not before Francy had written down the names of all those involved and placed the paper into a bottle which he sealed and put into the foundation. There were no more than one hundred persons present although reports at the time described the gathering as much greater. When the construction on the site was completed, the Canon unveiled and blessed the cross. Father Peter Maguire recited one decade of the rosary and they hastened away as fast as possible before they could catch their death of cold.

There was a lady in Bray, Celia O'Brien, who wrote some nice poetry and she composed these lines to commemorate the event:

A Hope Fulfilled

A youth stood on Bray Cualann's Strand,
Where Patrick vainly tried to land
He gazed upon the heights above
And thought of God and all His love
And of that love to tell the world,
He visioned there a flag unfurled.
When pondering mortals gain and loss
He knew he wanted there a cross.
His path was rough the way was long.
With love of God his heart beat strong,
Helping poor sinners on the road,
Often as blinding tears outflowed.
He clasped the cross.
God smiled upon the youthful dream,
Nothing too hard for him would seem.
So now the youth long since a man
Lifts up his priestly eyes to scan
Those selfsame heights and there so bright
In all its glory and its might
He sees the cross.

Celia O'Brien passed away not long ago. Canon Moriarty was to live a short one and a half years after the cross was placed there, he died on April 20th 1952. And now I'll come back to tell you about another famous person, that I've already mentioned very briefly.

FATHER JAMES HEALY

He was born in Dublin on December 15th. 1824, one of a family which numbered twenty three children (you see, his father was married twice!). Having obtained his early secondary education in Castleknock College he went to Maynooth where he continued his studies for the priesthood.

What momentous events in our history's making he must have witnessed in his early years! The poverty that abounded, the horrors that prevailed during the many outbreaks of cholera, O'Connell's Monster Meetings as he strove vainly for repeal of the Union and, most of all, the appalling ravages of the terrible hunger.

It was during a cholera outbreak in Dublin that the young priest was seen to lie down with the dying, in their disease-infested hovels, in order to hear their last confessions. He was also to be seen carrying a bundle of straw on his back to provide one of the innumerable victims with something to lie upon before they expired.

The poverty that existed is noted briefly in Memories of Father James Healy when it is recorded that, when the British Government increased the grant for Maynooth College from £8,000 to £30,000 per annum, that each student could obtain £20 a year which "enabled not a few to keep the spark of life in some aged parent, shivering by a mountain-side or bed ridden on the earthen floor". The famine, which set in immediately after Peel's bounty, and continued its desolating effects for several years, left "the class of people from whose ranks the priesthood mostly came unable to pay for a college course". It was Cardinal Cullen who moved him from Dublin to our growing town in the waning years of, the then Parish Priest's, Father Alexander Roche's life. Among his many initial duties was the celebration of the eight o'clock Mass in Kilmacanogue (St. Canoc's) and the twelve in Bray. Kilmacanogue was in Bray parish and the area, as well as the newly arrived curate, was described:

> *Father Healy knew his sheep and his sheep knew him. His weekly visit to this quaint village on the road to Wexford, situated between the great and smaller Sugarloaf mountains, was full of interest to him. The small chapel in which he said Mass was a relic of penal times and might be regarded as the successor of the ivy-mantled ruin fringed by the graves of rude forefathers, which formed a picturesque object adjacent. The steadfast faith and piety of its primitive people edified him; he entered into their little joys and sorrows; his cheerful smile and pleasant greeting won their hearts; and he soon knew the inside of every cabin as well as the gilded salons, in which he was equally welcome.*

The gilded salons referred to were Dublin Castle and the mansions of the Earl of Meath, Lord Monck, Lord Powerscourt and Mr. Putland where he attended many splendid dinners and entertained the nobility and their guests with his knowledge and ready wit.

Some samples of his humour and repartee, which was as sharp as a razor, are:

On hearing that a visiting priest, a Father Ring, had nearly drowned while swimming at Bray Head he retorted that they nearly had to call Bray Head Ringsend!

When dining at a dinner in the old home of Judge Philip Crampton, who was one of the judges at Daniel O'Connell's trial, and when all the guests were partaking of a generous measure of fine wines in a room where a large portrait of the teetotal and stern judge, who was long since dead, was hanging, someone was heard to exclaim "If he could look down at us now I wonder what he'd say?" to which Healy replied " Take care it's not up he'd have to look!" On hearing that one of his parishioners had been fiddling with a gun which went off injuring his toes and blowing off his shoe he exclaimed " Why this is a case of shoeaside!" Shortly after Sir William Wilde, who was slovenly and careless with his appearance, had been knighted one of Father Healy's acquaintances was telling him "I left Holyhead in a gale and came across the dirtiest night!" to which Healy retorted "It must have been Wilde!"

No matter how bad or cold the weather was he never wore an overcoat and when asked by a lady "Father Healy, you never wear a great coat!" he replied "No Madam, I never was!" .

He was in the habit of being collected from the residence of one of his noble acquaintances, where he had dined well, by a jarvey who was very fond of the drink. He said to the jarvey "drunk again Peter!" to which remark the jarvey replied "I'm a little that way myself father".

The litany of humour left behind by this famous priest is inexhaustible, but is overshadowed by his more serious side, which was that of a priest performing his priestly duties and caring for the spiritual (and sometimes material) needs of his flock. He was sent from Holy Redeemer to Little Bray where he was at first appointed Administrator and later Parish Priest.

It was in Little Bray that he entertained many important personages at what was described as his 'humble' table among whom were princes and prelates, peers and politicians and even on one occasion the Papal Envoy who was later to become Cardinal. He built St. Peter's School and carried out many improvements in the parish. Perhaps the greatest compliment was paid to him by a curate who ministered under him and who said :

The world, of which he was the ornament, knew him and idolised him. But the few acquainted with the beauty of his other and inner life of child-like faith and tender piety revered him and blessed him, not for his mental prowess only, but also, and more so, for his hidden goodness. The edifying cadences of his recitation of the "Hail! Holy Queen" after his daily Mass, and the soul stirring music of his Christmas morning preachings, still linger pleasantly in the mindful ears of his congregation at Little Bray. His cheery word, that so often sweetened the gifts of his open hand, is still treasured in the hearts of its poor.

He was transferred to Ballybrack where he died, Parish Priest. His wit continued right to the end. The last words he addressed to his curate were 'The doctors have been here; they have passed judgement, and left me no loophole for escape', and turning to his sister Mary he said 'Notice to quit.'

International Hotel

And while on his death bed his doctor commented to him
"you cough with more difficulty this morning,"

He replied,'
"Strange, for I have been practising all night!"

He died on October 28th 1894 aged seventy. His friend and devoted curate,
Father Burke, described his funeral:

> *His obsequies, in his parish church at Ballybrack, presented a*
> *spectacle of public mourning without a precedent, perhaps, in all our*
> *history. The Archbishop of Dublin, with his Cathedral Chapter, the*
> *Most Rev. Bishop Donnelly, and countless clergy, secular and regular*
> *(many of them from distant dioceses), the Protestant Archbishop of*
> *Dublin, the Venerable Archdeacon Scott, Rector of Bray, and the*
> *rectors of the surrounding parishes, the Lord Mayor of Dublin, the*
> *Chief Secretary for Ireland, representatives of the Lord Lieutenant and*
> *of ex. Viceroys, peers, judges, notabilities from all the professions, and*
> *the leading gentry and persons of distinction, vied with each other and*
> *with the peasants and the poor, who had flocked from all quarters, but*
> *especially from Little Bray, in offering the last sad token of their*
> *undying love to the dead priest, whose like they shall not look upon*
> *again.*

His funeral was the largest ever witnessed in Dublin at that time and it didn't
reach the cemetery until many hours after its scheduled arrival. There were
countless numbers waiting for the remains in the graveyard amongst whom
were Field-Marshal Lord Wolseley and the Duke of Teck. The following poem
is said to have voiced the feelings of his Protestant admirers and friends
towards him on his death :

> *'Toll the bell! a soul is passing*
> *From its mortal home of clay;*
> *Holy prayers, our voices breathing,*
> *Speed it on the heavenward way.*
> *Toll the bell ! the good priest dying*
> *Leaves in memories pure and fond*
> *Deeds of mercy never ending,*
> *Earthly treasures far beyond.*
> *Toll the bell ! no broken hearted*
> *Ever sought his help in vain;*
> *His, the word of sacred comfort,*
> *Bids the mourners smile again.*

'Toll the bell! the scene is holy;
Calm, in sleep of death , he lies;
Round him throng the great, the lowly,
In the solemn sacrifice.
Toll the bell! while sunbeams bursting
Through the autumn noontide sky,
Speak in tones of heavenly glory,
"Welcome to thy home on high !"

And you, dear reader, perhaps if you have the time, you might visit St. Peter's in Little Bray where you'll find in the porch a marble Holy Water font presented to the church, he loved so well, by his sister in his memory. Bless yourself and enter within and say a small prayer in thanksgiving for the life of Father James Healy.

DELGANY

Just a short distance south west of Bray Head and close to Greystones rests this beautiful and historic village in peaceful slumber. It's mentioned in the Annals of the Four Masters and is associated with Saint Mogoroc, who established a church there. Such a building would have been constructed from timber and therefore no trace remains of it to-day. The grandson of a British king, he lived for a time in Glendalough with our famous Saint Kevin, to whom he administered the last rites in 618. Another church replaced the early primitive cell-like structure, this time built from stone in the hope and expectation that it would withstand the test of time. Regrettably this was not to be, because of the tragic history that was to occur throughout Ireland, and the little church was in ruins by the early seventeenth century. To-day nothing remains of this structure except for the ancient cemetery that surrounded it. The history of the old building is well documented, although sometimes confusingly, in papal records and letters left to us by the Archbishops of Dublin. Many of the gravestones can still be seen and read, most are in a good state of preservation, perhaps because they are well sheltered from the wind. One of these memorials is the lower part of a large Celtic cross, the immensity of which is an indication of the great importance of the site as a very early Christian one and is perhaps proof that indeed it does date back to the time of Saint Kevin. The inscription on the cross, long faded by the winds of time and decipherable up to the mid nineteenth century, is in Irish and in English the translation reads *"Pray for Dicus and Maelodran the mason"*. A few paces from the remains of the cross, mind the nettles and tread softly on the hallowed ground, there is a protuberance which might indicate where the top part of the monument has been buried throughout the long centuries. I cannot but wonder at the strangeness of the broken granite stone and what awful force caused it to be split in two, no human hands could possess such strength, perhaps a ball from the mouth of a cannon was responsible for the foul desecration, if this be so then who was the miserable wretch who fired the shot?. The broken cross stands forever like a finger pointing to heaven in silent accusation.

When William of Orange came over to Ireland in 1691 and defeated the Irish, this was to change everything in our country, and in Delgany because one of officers was David Digues, a French Huguenot serving in La Caillemote's Regiment, who was to change his name to La Touche and whose grandson was to settle in Delgany in 1753 (where Delgany Golf Club now is). When the war between James and William was over, David entered into business as a banker in Dublin and his firm was known as La Touche Bank and situated on Cork

Hill. Although he was a banker he was recognised as being compassionate and charitable. It is said that when he went out of his home, he always first filled his pockets with shillings which he freely distributed to the poor as he passed them. When he was told that some of the beggars to whom he gave alms were spending his largesse on alcohol, he retorted "I know, but if my shilling falls right once in ten times that is enough". He died in 1745.

The La Touche family became numbered among the merchant princes of Dublin, and were recognised as prominent bankers and shrewd but honest businessmen (also associated with the development of the canals - Rathmines Bridge, in Dublin, is called La Touche Bridge). Peter La Touche came to dwell at Ballydonough in the Glen of The Downs and he changed the name from Ballydonough to Bellevue. It's no wonder that his interests strayed from commerce towards more pastoral and edifying pursuits, being surrounded by such beautiful scenery and woodlands that abound in that area. He began to devote his energies to horticulture and developed Bellevue into magnificent gardens and conservatories. The La Touche estate became the largest employer in Delgany, Greystones and the locality and inhabitants prospered. Peter La Touche was responsible for building the present Church of Ireland there in 1789 of which many of the stones came, regrettably, from the ancient ruined one. The building was designed by Whitmore Davis and above the entrance you find the La Touche crest. Inside there is a magnificent massive Carrera marble monument, sculpted by John Hickey, to the memory of Peter La Touche. The inscription over the memorial reads "Of Thy own, O my God, do I give unto Thee".

Would that all that passed in this apparently peaceful hamlet was of a spiritual nature. Unfortunately Delgany wasn't to escape the cruel and turbulent history of Ireland's past. In the year 1022 there was a great battle fought here between King Sitric (the Viking who was commemorated during the Dublin millennium celebrations) and the armies of Leinster when many thousands were slain. In the rising of 1641 there was more fighting and the old church was further damaged together with many of the surrounding dwellings. Much of the area was further subjected to cruel acts of barbarism when Cromwell's troops were to quench all resistance. His dreaded follower, Coote, scourged the countryside shortly afterwards.

In the year 1798 the inhabitants had great cause to regret its proximity to Newtownmountkennedy, where a Welsh regiment, the Ancient Britons, were quartered. These troops, together with supporters from the local Wicklow Militia, rode into the village and called to the abode of a Mr.Walsh who was recognised as a man of substantial wealth. Walsh was out on business at the time and the brave soldiers burnt his house and the rest of his property. A respectable family, the Ludlows, who were members of the Established Church and supported the Crown, employed a poor simple man named Coughlan who was seized by the troops, who then tied his arms to two of their horses and galloped with the unfortunate wretch for many miles, dragging him behind. The poor soul in consequence ended his days both an invalid in body as well as mind. Next they took a man by the name of Manren and brought him to Wicklow gaol where he was hanged. A large timid person, John Farrel, who was quite harmless and recently married was next taken and shot. His body was thrown into the small stream that flows near the village, where his poor remains lay for a long time, blocking the flow of the water; the inhabitants were too afraid to whisper a last prayer in his ear. They then shot a person by the name of Condron and then a Mr. Weafer, who was the local miller. After the day's sport they rode off to inflict their bloody presence elsewhere. These Welsh Britons and their supporters were never brought to justice in this world for their heinous crimes; instead they were rewarded by their country with honours.

The infamous General Lake, Commander in Chief of the Crown forces, was replaced by a more benevolent and far seeing General Cornwallis who, recognising the great suffering that prevailed after the rising, became aware that if Ireland was to be pacified he would have to do so with a 'kid glove' otherwise the fighting would continue. The Establishment formed an organisation called The Society for Promoting the Comforts of the Poor with Cornwallis as its president, in order to try and alleviate the miserable and wretched circumstances of the peasantry, subsequent to the harsh punishment resulting from the rising's suppression. One of the many institutions that came into existence through the Society was the establishment of shops that were the forerunners of our co-ops. One such institution was opened in Delgany in 1799.

Every labourer who was resident in the parish for a minimum of two years was entitled to use the shop provided he had a recommendation from any gentleman or farmer in the area, supported by a note from the local Church of Ireland clergyman. The privilege could be withdrawn through idleness, misconduct, or by selling any article purchased in the shop. The goods available included almost every article in general use among the poor for food, medicine or clothing, and they were sold for a little above cost and for cash only. It was reckoned that the savings to the purchasers was as much as one third of the price that they would have to normally pay in other retail outlets. The premises were open every day, except Sunday, from sunrise to sunset. Among the common articles purchased at the time were milk, butter, bacon, salt, herrings, oatmeal, groats, rice, barley, wheatmeal, tea, sugar, treacle, vinegar, mustard, pepper, soap, candles, sulphur, flax, wool, flannel, coarse stockings, wooden and leather shoes, shifts, shirts, aprons, nitre, cream of tartar, glauber salts, ginger and umbrellas! Even in those days they couldn't stand the rain!

The ready-made articles were partly supplied by girls at a school which was established by the same organisation and partly by the poor of the neighbourhood.

The shop was annexed to a small house and all customers were served at the door by a man and his wife who lived on the premises and who ran the business. The man was also a gardener and no doubt also worked in the La Touche estate nearby. They were paid by having the house rent free and being allowed to take anything from the shop that was essential for their existence. The account books were kept and written up by a youth of fourteen who was badly crippled in an accident. These books also contained the names of all purchasers and each article sold was carefully noted in a large Morocco leather bound journal.

Because of the demand created by the shop a small factory was opened in the village to make clothes. Women and girls of the area were taught how to stitch, sew and cut the material that was provided to them and in return they were rewarded with a small wage, a meal each day, and a fire in the room that they occupied while they were working.

The price of some of the items on sale were, salt, three farthings a pound; soap, six pence halfpenny; butter, one shilling and sixpence; bacon, six and a half pence; meat, one and a half pence; tobacco, a penny halfpenny an ounce; tea (a great luxury in those days), five shillings a pound; wooden shoes, four shillings and ten pence; leather shoes, nine shillings.

A further word about the sale of umbrellas. I quote from a contemporary tract "It may excite surprise that umbrellas should be one of articles of the assortment, but they are sometimes purchased by the poor; and a labouring man has been known to save money from the ale-house, in order to enable him to procure this protection against a rainy Sunday for his wife and daughters".

It was not surprising that most of the inhabitants of Delgany, as well as Bray, went barefoot because of the price of shoes. The average wage of a labourer was about four shillings a week. A whole weeks work for one pair of shoes!

The Society was also instrumental in setting up schools - the exact records for the period in Delgany have been lost or destroyed but those from an area further south are still available and it is thought that that they would be similar to those for here. The average description of the pupils scholarly ability was, Cypherers, 19%; Writers not cyphering, 19%; Readers not writing, 18%; Spellers only, 27% and Learning the alphabet, 16%.

In order to raise additional funds for their various worthy causes the Society issued appeals to those with wealth as follows;

> *You have long felt the necessity of some effectual provision for the poor; the present scarcity and dearness of provisions, and want of employment, have increased the distress and misery of many that are inclined to be industrious, and multiplied public beggary so much beyond what it has been at any former period, that the time seems now come, wherein every possible personal exertion, and every pecuniary help can be procured, are loudly called for, to aid in endeavouring to apply adequate remedies to the present evils, and prevent their recurrence in future.*

The funds raised as a result of this appeal were returned to the donors eventually from the profits made in the shop.

The Society didn't last long as soon it was involved in scandals when there were rows over misappropriation of funds. There is a record however indicating that the shop might have continued its existence up to 1815 when Atkinson, in The Irish Tourist, noted that there was a straw hat and a bonnet factory in the village, with prices ranging at the time from one to thirty shillings.

Well that's all for Delgany for the present. Those who dwell there since have lived in peace and tranquillity and give grateful thanks in Peter La Touche's church and in the nearby Carmelite convent for the wonders of nature that smile on them. So the next time you visit this delightful place, perhaps you'll find a moment to quietly ponder and reflect on its history, while you might enjoy the hospitality and refreshments provided by the Wicklow Arms and the Delgany Inn.

Now let us take another look at another famous person who was familiar with Bray.

HENRY GRATTAN

Not far from Bray and in close proximity to Powerscourt is Tinnehinch, which was once the home of one of Ireland's most famous politicians in the eighteenth century, Henry Grattan.

He was born in 1746, studied law in Trinity College, was called to the bar in 1772 and, like most lawyers of that time and many still to-day, became interested in politics. In 1775 he was elected to the Irish Parliament and it was around then that he first came to know and love Bray and its neighbourhood. There was great dissatisfaction in Ireland, not because we were ruled by a foreign power, but because the Parliament in London could overrule any laws or decisions made in Ireland. There were severe restrictions imposed on Ireland which prevented Irish manufacturers and exporters competing equally with their British counterparts.

Events outside began to affect what was happening here, the American War of Independence and the French Revolution. Wars outside Ireland stripped this country of a regular standing army. There was little protection at sea from privateers preying on shipping around our coasts and no defence of property or the interests of those who owned our land if the Irish peasants rose up against them or if there was a French invasion. In order to correct this the landlords and gentry formed the Irish Volunteers which was described by Grattan, who became one of its leading figures, as 'the armed property of the nation'. This force was comprised of men of substance, landlords and wealthy merchants. From its original intention of protecting the property of the rich, the popular movement was to change into a politically conscious organisation, with new democratic and sometimes radical attitudes being learned from America and France. The British Government and the power of Dublin Castle were unable to proscribe the Volunteers, as they had become so numerous and popular that it was too late to outlaw the organisation without risking an armed rebellion which would have the support of all the people.

The Irish Parliament, with Grattan and the Volunteers, soon began to exercise their powerful voice in the hope of getting 'Free Trade' from the Government in London. Initially the polite request was refused when Grattan presented the motion in 1780 and 1781. The British government was now faced with the very real possibility of losing Ireland, and realising this they agreed to pass the bill for Free Trade when it was again presented in 1782. This was his greatest moment and his finest year. He married in 1782 and a grateful Irish Parliament and people purchased Tinnehinch (formerly an inn) for his residence. Grattan's new home was described in 1814:

I can assure you that for some minutes the feelings excited within me were too strong for expression. I was enraptured with the situation of the man's dwelling, but still more with the recollection of himself and our dear country, which, as he said, "he had watched in her cradle and conducted to her tomb.

There was some uncertainty and doubt about the Free Trade that was given. Could it be taken away from them at some time? The Irish Parliament pondered this possibility and they soon realised that what they had attained was only temporary. So Grattan and his parliament decided to try and have it copperfastened by proposing that 'Only Kings, Lords and Commons of Ireland could make laws for Ireland'. This was granted in 1783 by the British Parliament and intended and promised to be enshrined in the statutes and laws of Britain and Ireland forever. We now had independence, or so we thought.

Seafront and Bray Head

Grattan and his parliament, and indeed the establishment were beginning to recognise the terrible injustice of the Penal Laws which excluded Catholics from participating in the practice of the professions and it was partly due to his influence that some of these unjust laws were relaxed. He was quite liberal towards Catholics, although it is believed that he would never have entertained the idea that they be permitted in Parliament.

79

He dwelt in peace and contentment, attending the independent parliament in College Green and strolling along the banks of the Dargle, admiring the beauty that nature had endowed on the area, at weekends. His peace was soon to be shattered and his life changed for the worse by the rising of 1798. Although he was never involved in either planning or supporting this he was strongly suspected by the Castle authorities and miserable informers of doing so. One of his friends and a prominent member of the United Irishmen, Arthur O'Connor, was arrested for high treason in England in the company of Father Cogley, both en route to France in order to obtain support from the Revolutionary Government for the rising in Ireland that was imminent. O'Connor prevailed on Grattan to travel to London and to appear on his behalf as a defence witness at the trial. Grattan did what his friend requested and O'Connor was acquitted. Father Cogley was found guilty and hanged. While Grattan was in London at this time the rising in Ireland broke out and he was arrested. In the meantime, while all this was going on, the yeomanry and militia were rampaging and pillaging throughout Ireland and they happened to be in the vicinity of Tinnehinch where Mrs. Grattan and her household were fearful for their lives. They destroyed some of her garden and threatened her in a most abusive manner. The children's tutor was present and they expressed a wish to hang him and then to burn her house. Lord Powerscourt, fortunately, was nearby and he prevailed on the undisciplined 'warriors' to desist from their bullying behaviour. Because of this the family immediately fled to Dublin and from there went to North Wales, where they awaited the outcome of Grattan's trial. Shortly after he was judged not guilty and then rejoined his family.

He didn't sit in the Irish Parliament again until 1800 when, in January of that year, he delivered the most eloquent and forceful attack against the Act of Union. The MPs who supported him, and the people of Dublin, gave him a tumultuous reception and an extract from a contemporary letter written by the wife of the Archbishop of Cashel to Earl Macartney, both of whom were opponents of Grattan, described the event as follows:

> *I hope Mr. Grattan is a little afraid of his head. He got out of one scrape miraculously* (obviously referring to his trial). *However I trust he is aware that miracles don't happen every day. This amiable idol was carried all about Sackville Street, Rutland Square etc. etc, the day before yesterday in his sedan chair by a most tumultuous mob, with shoutings, huzzaings and applauses enough to rend the skies.*

Notwithstanding the support for Grattan from the majority who were opposed to the Union, the Act was eventually passed, through bribery, in 1800 and came into force in 1801. He was defeated and retired to Tinnehinch and Bray.

From 1805, until his death in 1820, he sat in Westminster during which period he eventually accepted the Union and didn't support the efforts of Daniel O'Connell to have it repealed. He did, however, speak out in favour of Catholic Emancipation up to the time he died. Towards the end of his life he was assailed with sombre and depressing sentiments of which he wrote :

> *Solitude is bad. I have tried Tinnahinch for twenty years. It leads to melancholy, to a sort of madness. You think of your vexations, your age. Society should always be in your power. An old man cannot enjoy solitude. He has found out the rogueries of Fortune. Nor will reading supply the want. I would live in a house full of society, to which I might escape from myself. I was called the Spirit of the Dargle. I found out that a man's worst companion is himself.*

Henry Grattan's remains lie far from his home, beside his beloved Dargle, in North Wicklow. He is buried in Westminster Abbey, London, at the feet of a statue, in white marble, of his enemy the infamous Lord Castlereagh.

KILMACANOGUE

Not far from Bray and close to Delgany rests this quiet sleepy hamlet consisting of two shops, one public house renowned for its liquid refreshment and hospitality to strangers, and one church. Its present appearance belies its past.

The village gets its name from Saint Canoc (Moconoc) who was a companion of St. Patrick and perhaps a brother of Mogoroc who founded the ancient church in Delgany. His feast day is 19th of December but there are some records giving this as February 11th. Canoc lived here where he founded a monastic settlement. The son of an Irish chieftain, he was born in Wales around the time of Saint Patrick and spent his life establishing schools and churches in Ireland and Wales.

The population of the area to-day is very small but that was not the case in the past. In the year 1766 there were 660 souls living there compared with 730 in Bray. In 1834 the numbers had increased to around 2,800 and Bray 3,300. The area was badly decimated by the great hunger of 1846 to 1850 (the drills on the Sugarloaf can be seen during a dry summer where the people tried vainly to grow potatoes) and it never recovered. Another cause for the reduction in population was the fact that the railway followed the coast through Bray and Greystones instead of going inland.

The ruins of an old ivy-covered church rest in tranquil slumber beneath the mountain and is surrounded by an ancient cemetery which contains the remains of many of our ancestors who once lived in Bray. Some of the stones date back to the 12th. century but the church was a total ruin by the early 17th. In papal documents of 1430 the building is mentioned with the name of the priest given as Father Cornelius Byrne. Later, in 1610, there is again mention of the church then falling into decay.

In the cemetery there are many tombstones which bear the names of Bray families, dating as far back as the early 1600s and hidden, beneath the ground, there lie many others that go back further. Bray hadn't a Catholic cemetery until St. Peter's was opened in 1843 and the burial grounds at Old Connaught and here were used. The cemetery has unfortunately been vandalised, like most others, by louts and ignorant layabouts, resulting in many fine memorial stones being broken. It is now necessary to padlock the gate but the key is available, on enquiry, for visitors. The secured gate proves to be of no hindrance to these Philistines as they are agile enough to scale the wall with ease. Among the many interesting inscriptions on the graves are, In memory of Gunner Martin

Byrne killed on active service in France 25 September 1916; Patrick Gannon 40 years farm steward in Kilruddery, this memorial erected by Reginald, Earl of Meath; William Delahoide 19 June 1831, 51 years faithful servant in Hollebrook, Sir George Hudson erected this stone in 1844 and many others.

It was from here that Father Christopher Callaghan came to Bray in 1792 to open our tiny 'chapel' on Main Street. He lived in Kilmacanogue, became parish priest of both Bray and Kilmacanogue until his death in 1823 when he was succeeded by Rev. James Canon Doyle. It was Father Doyle who built the new church in Kilmacanogue in 1824 and the one on Bray's main street in 1826, where he was buried. His successor, Rev. Alexander Roche, had intended to place a memorial stone over his grave to read as follows:-

Beneath this stone is laid
the body of
The Reverend James Doyle
who was born in the parish of Rathdrum, A.D.1779.
Ordained priest 11th. June, 1808
Appointed to the United Parishes of Newbridge and Baroniskea
A.D.1814
Where he laboured for ten years
Instructing the ignorant and reclaiming sinners
Was translated to this Parish, A.D. 1824,
Where he began the Building of this Church, Ministered for two Years
and Seven Months, a Zealous, Pious Pastor of the Flock of Christ and
Departed this life in June, 1826.
May he rest in peace.
Whose successor, the Reverend Alexander Roche, P.P, Vicar Forane.
Set up this Commemorative Tablet A.D. 1858.
Laus Deo Semper

Father Roche died before he could set up this memorial and so Father Doyle has a simple inscription on his grave (in Holy Redeemer) just giving his name and date of death. On the other hand there is a fine marble memorial to Father Roche inside St. Mochonog's where he is buried.

Down through the centuries, Kilmacanogue was to witness the clans of the O'Tooles and O'Byrnes as they sped to fight against the English Planters in the Pale. During the rising of 1641, two ladies, a Mrs. Smithson and her maid were abducted from Stillorgan and brought here where they were murdered. Shortly thereafter Cromwell and his army passed through the area and that was the end of any resistance from the O'Tooles and the O'Byrnes. Their lands were taken from them for good.

That reminds me of a story of a mountainy man known as the 'King O'Toole'. He reared lean sheep far up on the hills passed the Sugarloaf and lived among them in a makeshift shelter. Once a year he'd take his stock to market and sell whatever surplus he had and then, with coins ringing in his pocket, he would head for the nearest hostelry where he would quench a year's thirst. After this, with his stout shepherd's stick under his arm, he would walk all the way to the estate of Lord Powerscourt and proceed to beat on the mansion's door shouting all the while 'Get out of my house!' The Powerscourts were well used to this annual performance and paid the 'King' little heed, knowing that he would soon desist from his disturbing behaviour when he sobered up.

The Sugarloaf, beneath which the village lies, was known as Sliabh Cualann (Slieve Cullen) and later as Giltspear down through the centuries until recent times when the name was anglicised. The mountain served as a marker for all those travelling along the east coast. It was also a sign post for the pilgrims and scholars that travelled to and from the monastic city of Glendalough. Glendalough! The mention of the name brings visions to the reader of saints and holy people treading a path through Kilmacanogue on their way to St. Kevin's and St. Laurence O'Toole's hallowed ground - but wait while I quote to you an extract from a letter in the year 1215 from the Archbishop of Tuam (Felix O' Ruadhain) to Pope Innocent the Third:

> that holy church in the mountains was from early times held in great
> reverence on account of St. Kevin who lived there as a hermit, it is now
> so deserted and desolate and has been so for forty years, that from
> being a church it has become a den of thieves and a pit of robbers, and
> because of the deserted and desolate wilderness there are more
> murders committed in that valley than in any other part of Ireland.

The worthy prelate's description was not correct and the reason why he wrote this calumny was that he hoped that the Pope would appoint him to take control of Glendalough. All those dwelling in Kilmacanogue and those passing through on their way to the Seven Churches at the time, were, as they are to-day, very good people.

ENNISKERRY

Often described as a quaint 'Alpine' style mountain village - this small hamlet has been a favourite venue for excursions by visitors to Bray for more than two centuries. A wonderful description of it is given by a French aristocrat who fled the Revolution and Terror and kept his head on his shoulders, Le Chevalier de La Tocnaye, in 1796:

> *"The innkeeper at Enniskerry is a representative of the O'Tooles who owned this territory in the far past and who lost their lands because they refused to submit to the English yoke. He has taken for sign the arms of the new proprietors. If ever the exiles return to France, and if their estates are not returned to them, I am certain of this, that it is not on my own lands that I shall become innkeeper".*

The arms referred to by him are still displayed on the front of the Powerscourt Arms Hotel; it continues to cater for visitors, and is famed for its hospitality to strangers, its good food and high standard of liquid nourishment. The hotel was destroyed by a fire in 1894 but thankfully the innkeeper at the time, Mr. Buckley, rebuilt it soon afterwards. A guidebook in the early 1900s has this to day of it :

> *An important village in the Parish of Powerscourt, about four and a half miles from Bray Railway Station, in the Barony and Union of Rathdown and Catholic Diocese of Dublin and Protestant Diocese of Glendalough. It is the head of a Petty Sessional District. This is the most beautiful district in all Ireland. No language can describe it. Every man, woman and child should see it; and owing to the kindness of the proprietor of the estate, Lord Powerscourt, visitors to the Powerscourt Arms Hotel are afforded every opportunity of viewing the superb beauty of the district, which would require a well spent week to explore.*

Nearly one hundred years ago the village was as self-sufficient as Bray was at the time; it had everything that was required to exist on its own with a population of over two hundred. Amongst them there was Jim Breheney the local butcher, Bill Walsh, who was the blacksmith (his forge is still there); Mick Reilly ran the post office, John Doyle sold and repaired shoes, Dick Brew was the local doctor who cured all their ailments (Dr. Michael Kenny, now retired, is there), Mick Tallon was grocer and he also baked bread, Hannah Buckley also looked after a grocery combined with a draper's shop. Dan Chambers was the sergeant in the Royal Irish Constabulary barracks and he had four other

members to help him maintain law and order; Father Michael Ivers was the Parish Priest and he had Father Carroll and Father Mc Grath to assist him, two other doctors resided there - Dr. Arthur Price and Dr. Bill Ross; John Windsor delivered post in all weathers and in those days there was a mountain of snow in the winter. In charge of the Church of Ireland school was Percy Steed and his opposite number in the Catholic school was Christy O'Rourke.

When Canon Alexander Roche was P.P of Bray, one of his curates was Father Thomas O'Dwyer and it was part of that poor curate's duties to travel by horseback to Enniskerry to celebrate Mass. Perhaps a pleasant experience on the road in summertime but terrible in those Victorian winters when temperatures were nearly always sub zero and when there was a lot of snow on the ground. There was no Catholic church there at the time and Mass was celebrated in a barn belonging to the Widow Dixon. It was Father O'Dwyer who was instrumental in building the Church of the Immaculate Heart of Mary which was opened in 1859. Father O'Dwyer became the first parish priest in the same year and he ministered to his flock until his death in 1887. On the day of the dedication, of the church the jarvies of Bray introduced a special low fare of fourpence (two new pence) for the journey to the village. Canon Roche died a few weeks after the dedication which was performed by the Archbishop of Cashel. The Archbishop of Dublin, Dr. Cullen later to become Cardinal, laid the foundation stone in 1858. The foundation stone of the Church of Ireland, St. Patrick's, was laid the year before, in 1857, but it was not consecrated until 1863. The ceremony of laying the foundation stones of both churches was performed with the use of beautifully-crafted trowels made from Wicklow silver. Silver mined in Wicklow was very fashionable in Victorian Ireland. The trowel used for the Church of the Immaculate Heart of Mary had an ivory carved cross in the handle which was made from a piece of a yew tree traditionally believed to have been planted by St. Kevin. I wonder where the trowel is now! Maybe in the Archbishop's palace in Dublin.

Before leaving Enniskerry I must tell you about George the Fourth's visit here in 1821. It was a big event for Ireland, with all sorts of famous people vying with one another to entertain the King so that they might be rewarded with his recognition of their importance. Everything was prepared for the regal presence in the mansion of Powerscourt, a specially-built throne was constructed to bear the weight of the royal visitor, the kitchens and wine cellars were overflowing with every sort of luxurious mouth-watering delicacies and the grounds and gardens decorated with all the rainbow colours that nature's bounty could display. The great attraction at Powerscourt is, of course, the waterfall which cascades down from a great height into a stream which eventually becomes the Dargle River and flows through Bray. The water from this attraction is filtered by the heather and bog of the mountain before tumbling over the rocky height and entering the crystal-clear pool at its base. In order to make the cascade more spectacular, a dam at the top was built, at great trouble and expense, and it was planned that at a given signal the deluge would be released for the thrill and amazement of George. All this planning and preparation came to naught, however, as the king wasn't interested in looking at the waterfall or any other attraction on the estate. He was satiated with the food and wine with which he overindulged himself and was incapable of proceeding to witness the dam being broken and the immense deluge of the released flood cascading into the pool far below.

Thinking of Bray and the area surrounding calls to mind another small hamlet not too far away. Rest awhile and I'll tell you about it.

NEWTOWNMOUNTKENNEDY

What a long name! but those dwelling there have simplified it by referring to it as 'Newtown' (I wonder was there ever an 'Oldtown-mountkennedy?'). Anyway the 'town' or village gets its name from an Alderman Kennedy who lived there in the seventeenth century, and who was knighted, during the Restoration, by Charles the Second. It is described in a guide book, nearly one hundred years ago, as "a small market town in the parish of Upper Newcastle, about two miles from Newcastle station on the Dublin and South Eastern Railway and three miles from Delgany and about twenty miles from Dublin. It is the head of a Petty Sessional Division and in the Union of Rathdrum. The scenery in the district is charming and a number of country gentry have built residences of a very high class in the immediate neighbourhood."

The Church of Ireland building is most beautiful with a tower of very handsome proportions and the Catholic Church, dedicated to St. Joseph, is built in the cruciform style and capable of accommodating a congregation of 600. The foundation stone was laid in 1860 and the church was enlarged in 1907.

In the course of some research into the effects of the dreadful Hunger on the area I was most fortunate to have an interview with an elderly gentleman who had lived there in excess of ninety summers and who has long since gone to God. He remembered the days when the twentieth century was in its infancy, and imparted information to me about the people who dwelt there at that time.

Mr. and Mrs. Kavanagh were in charge of the Catholic Primary Schools and a Miss Coulter looked after the Protestant one. Michael Reilly was in the Post Office selling stamps with the new king's head on them (Queen Victoria was dead and her postage stamps no longer in circulation). In the local Royal Irish Constabulary station there was Sergeant Billy Adams and four constables to keep law and order, and to nip any sign of sedition in the bud. The Church of Ireland rector was Reverend Craig and the Catholic curate was Father Peter Early, who as his name suggests was never late for Mass. There were no less that eight magistrates, so that miscreants could be tried and promptly sentenced and removed from society without any delay. Among those stern upholders of the law were Dr. Archer of Delgany, Major Cunningham of Kildreenan, Major Wellesley and Judge Moore of Drummin. Important people, with important and pompous names to suit them residing in the area were Count Peter Bastigo, Captain Henry Cooper, Captain Henry Seagrave, Major Charles Tottenham and Mrs. Patience Gilbert. They wined and dined with other gentry, among whom were Miss Martin of Glendarragh, Thomas Byrne of Kildreenan, William Corbett of Springfarm, John Hudson of Kilquade, Art Irwin of Prospect, John Loverock of Springmount and Mrs. Isabella Stamper of Monaline.

Thirsty travellers could refresh themselves in Henry Newell's hostelry while their horses were being watered, and in competition with Henry there was Tom Short (who was quite tall) and Paddy Redmond who was also a blacksmith. Most of the ales came from the brewery in Bray. Dr. Lynch, physician and surgeon, medical officer for the dispensary district cured them all of their ailments until old age finally dispatched them. And watching everything that went on was Bill Gilbert, the terror and scourge of the area and a thorn in every side, who was the local Income Tax collector.

In the rising of 1798 Newtownmountkennedy was to suffer the most appalling barbarities perpetrated by the local Newtown Mounted Yeomen supported by a troop of the notorious Ancient Britons from Bray. The litany of names of those tortured and murdered, mostly by their fellow Irishmen, are too numerous to set down here, but I will mention only one important name - Michael Neil, who was a well known member of the United Irishmen. He was brought to Newtown, where he was incarcerated in the Market House, which was filled with other prisoners, and there he was subjected to the cruellest torture before he was brutally murdered. There is a small stone erected opposite to the Catholic Church, in his memory, but perhaps his greatest epitaph was written by Br. Luke Cullen, the great 1798 historian, as follows:

> *Reader, whoever you may be, if ever you go to Newtownmountkennedy, as you go from Dublin and cross the little arch that spans the rivulet that waters the town, look to the right, and between you and the next tavern kept by a Mr. Maguire you will see the spot where the inhuman butchery of Michael Neil, of Upper Newcastle, was perpetrated by Newtown Yeomen and Ancient Britons, on the 1st. of June 1798. May he rest in Peace.*

I wonder why there are no other memorials in the village to those others who fell in the 'battle' or to those who were executed. (I'll tell you a little more about the unfortunate events that occurred in the next chapter.)

To-day Newtownmountkennedy rests in tranquillity, and I think that the fact that it is bypassed by the new dual carriageway is a blessing. If the reader wishes to relax, I recommend that a visit to the village be made and its hospitality sampled. There are some splendid shops selling the most colourful plants and antiques, as well as nice establishments where liquid refreshment can be imbibed in pleasant surroundings.

BRAY AND THE RISING OF 1798

Just over twenty years before 1798, the American colonies had dared to challenge the right of Britain to rule them, and to the surprise of all, after a long and bloody conflict, the colonists won their independence. Tom Paine wrote the Rights of Man and the then preposterous idea was sown that all men might have been born equal. In France, a scarce ten years before, there occurred another bloody revolution, this time perhaps more dangerous because it involved the near elimination of all the aristocracy and the murder of the French king and his family. These new ideas spread and there was nowhere more receptive to receive them than the peasants of Ireland and a large number of liberal minded landlords. It was just over one hundred years before when the Irish armies had been defeated and exiled following the battles of the Boyne, Aughrim and Limerick. The memory of those defeats and the confiscation of the land was alive and festering. The United Irishmen were founded.

Life in Bray was as it always was, quiet and peaceful, the poor people worked if they could find work, they laughed and cried, sometimes they were hungry but that was normal as it was all that they were used to. The population in the area, including the immediate surrounding countryside, was about five thousand wretched souls. There was a small garrison of regular troops in the town, just to keep an eye on them, and immediately outside, to the north at Loughlinstown, there were many thousands of fellow Irishmen from the infamous North Cork Militia, Longford Regiment, Cavan, Lord Donaghmore's, South Mayo, Downshire, Londonderry, Louth, Clare, Meath, 5th. Dragoons and many others.

The drums began to beat and the fifes began to sound as they played the tune 'Croppies Lie Down'. Small flames grew into large conflagrations as county by county rose and were subdued, leaving a countryside laid waste, gibbets filled and gaols overflowing. The last place to be pacified was Wicklow where all had been reasonably quiet until now.

In Newtownmountkennedy there was a large camp of militia and the Wicklow insurgent leader, General Joseph Holt, a member of the Established Church, attacked the town on May 30th but was defeated. The Militia subsequently got inebriated and flogged, tortured and pitch-capped many in the village.

Bray was commencing to become involved. Poor Father Christopher Callaghan, whose little chapel was a small thatched cabin behind the main street, had to flee Major Hardy's regulars belonging to the local garrison. He was given asylum by the Earl of Meath in Kilruddery, just outside the town.

At Kilquade, the Catholic church was razed by the troops. Were the ordinary plain people of Bray involved ? Was John Byrne aged seventeen and Myles Doyle aged nineteen among those whose only epitaph was a short note in The Dublin Evening Post on July 7th as follows:

> *Seventeen men employed by a brewer, eloped from thence, one of whom left behind him, a written note to his employer, stating his reason for going away, which he said was in consequence of a notice from his officer (a rebel) ordering him to join his ranks immediately.*

Did they ever return, or do their bones lie with others in unmarked graves beneath a shroud of heather in the hills outside Bray, beneath the shadow of The Sugarloaf?

General Craig had, on the instructions of the cruel and infamous Lake, who was Commander in Chief of the king's forces, posted notices in Bray and throughout Wicklow, ordering all 'rebels' to surrender their arms. The time usually given to give up such arms was seven to ten days, but on this occasion it was a mere two. The terms usually given were a general amnesty, and for anyone found 'under arms' subsequently, it was the death penalty. It is generally reputed that the time given for the Wicklow insurgents was deliberately short so that Lake's army would have a legitimate cause for executing the remaining United-men who were at large.

In Bray, Captain Edwards commanded the Bray Infantry. Now Edwards is thought to have been a kind and sensible sort of person, a descendant of an old and honourable Bray family who had come here from Wales during the reign of Charles the Second and who subsequently owned Oldcourt Castle. He was also one of our local magistrates. Of course he opposed the insurgents, which is why he wore the king's uniform, otherwise he would have joined the United-men reputed to have been in the town. Major Joseph Hardy, of the garrison commanding the loyalist troops in Wicklow and Bray, suspected that Edwards was sympathetic towards the insurgents, the reason being that he was not seen to be ill-treating the poor people living here. He knew that he would still live here in Bray when all this butchery was over, unlike Hardy who had no family or friends in the area. The authorities in Dublin Castle were asked to remove Edwards from his command, and there is little doubt that his life was endangered. The fact that he was a magistrate, a member of the Established Church and wore the king's uniform, didn't mean that he was free from the savagery of the regular troops. Hardy's boast was that "violence, rigour, house burnings, half hanging and flogging were the only means of effecting a surrender". Edwards is said to have pledged himself to protect the people of

Bray from Hardy's Regulars, but yet he convinced the Castle that he wasn't sympathetic towards the 'rebels'.

It was Edwards who rode out and went up into the hills outside Bray, where he accepted the surrender of many United-men. They were treated with respect, were not asked to inform on their comrades and all were pardoned. Many more would have surrendered, but the time given to them had expired and they had to flee further into the hills of Wicklow. Among those who would have surrendered if they had been given enough time, were General Joseph Holt and Michael Dwyer. Holt's contribution to the rising was to a great extent ignored by local historians, unlike Dwyer who has been glorified with exaggerated folk hero worship.

A respectable farmer, Holt was a member of the Established Church, and commander of the insurgents in Wicklow from July until November 1798. He joined the United Irishmen on the 10th of May in that year after his house was burnt by crown forces. Many came to join his well-armed and disciplined band, in consequence of which he was to be of the greatest threat to the troops and wealthy landowners in north Wicklow. After having fought a long guerrilla war in the area with great success, he eventually surrendered to Lord Powerscourt, Richard the fourth viscount, who commanded the Powerscourt Cavalry and the Glencree Pioneers, on the bank of our lovely Dargle, just outside Bray. A measure of his success is indicated by the fact that, out of all counties, Wicklow received the second largest payment of compensation to loyalists for property destroyed. He was thirty-nine years old when he was transported to Botany Bay. As the ship carrying him and eighty others passed by Bray and the Wicklow Hills he said "If I had known the misery of this vessel, no lord or lady would have influence enough to induce me to surrender". He returned to Ireland, after being pardoned by the Governor of New South Wales, and became a publican in Dublin where he died in May 1826.

In Mr. & Mrs. Hall's Ireland there is this to be said of him:-

> *He contrived to keep his guerrillas together for several months after the troubles had terminated elsewhere, the peculiar nature of the country being favourable to his plans, the people being universally friendly to him, and every hill and valley furnishing some place of secrecy and security- at least for a time. A price was set upon his head; his every motion was tracked by spies; yet he managed to escape. His history is singular and striking; he was a man of courage and enterprise, and of sagacity and prudence very rare in those days. He executed some very brilliant movements; and on several occasions*

destroyed parties of the King's troops. He first assembled his band in the Devil's Glen; thence removed his quarters to Luggelaw, and subsequently to Glendalough; but he was soon compelled to take to the hills, driven like grouse from hill to hill, from whence he continually rushed with a rapidity resembling that of their torrents 'down upon the vale' certain to leave his mark behind him, his animosity being principally directed against the yeomanry. In the course of two months he was at the head of nine hundred and sixty men - all Wicklow men. His first regular battle was at Ballyellis, where he slew a party of the Ancient Britons to the number of perhaps a hundred, which he magnifies into three hundred and seventy. This success rapidly augmented his forces and by the month of July the number on his roll was 13,780; but the majority were evidently attracted to his camp by the beeves he had killed and baked ; for in one day no fewer than 2,500 deserted. His escapes were often marvellous ; on one occasion having been wounded in the head, and finding himself watched by some police, he went boldly up to them and asked which way the army had gone, affirming that the rebels had robbed him of his horse and hat. They pitied his misfortune, and said it was lucky for him it was no worse. At length, wearied out, and utterly hopeless of any termination to his career but death upon the gallows, he resolved to surrender; being urged chiefly thereto by the appalling position in which he found himself; to quote his own words:- ' I had not only to watch the movements of His Majesty's forces, in constant hunt after me, to guard against the machinations of the spy, the informer, and blood money man, but also treason in my own camp.

Holt mentions the hospitality given to him by the people of Wicklow when he was being hunted. He came to a farmhouse whose sole occupants were a poor old woman and her daughter:

They brought me hot water to bathe my feet, and clean stockings and linen, and took my own and washed them. Then they gave me oat cakes and buttermilk, which after I had eaten, they shewed me a comfortable bed, where I slept for several hours

They had believed that he had been killed and they grieved at his death. Having informed them of his identity, they expressed their joy at his safety and their pride in having him as their guest.

Wicklow, described in 1798 as a 'mass of rebellion' was now silent. The rising was soon over but the suffering of those who had been defeated increased. Ireland had again been vanquished but would rise again.

SAM NAYLOR

During the 1939-1945 war, Irish ships ventured forth from our ports to try and maintain commerce, trade and industrial supplies which were so essential for our infant state. Independence for the twenty-six counties was won only a short seventeen years past. These ships, like those of Spain, Sweden, Portugal and others, were neutral in the dreadful conflict that was occurring. Merchant vessels belonging to these non-combatant countries proudly carried their nation's flag, and also had it painted on the hull of both starboard and port side, so that they could easily be identified as neutrals by British and German submarines, warships and bombers. None of these merchant ships carried any armament and so they were defenceless against the smallest act of aggression. One could be forgiven in assuming that they were safe at sea and that the only enemy they had to face were the elements and the hazards of navigation. Oh would that such was the case! Many Irish ships were to sail from their neutral home ports never to return. Many of the crew bade, unknowingly, a final farewell to their families, as they departed through their front doors, their duffel bags packed for the last time, as they faced towards the hungry sea.

Neutral ships were torpedoed, bombed and strafed during this terrible war, perhaps through errors of identification, some through deliberate cold-blooded acts of terrorism. They had no radar, so they depended on the senses that God gave them to maintain a good watch, collisions in the dark occurred and many struck mines. The proud and lovely vessels met an untimely end and lie on the bed of the oceans with some of their crews who, at the time, went unremembered and mostly unmourned, except for their immediate families.

It was early in September 1941 in Bray. The weather was warm and the days long. People talked about the 'Emergency' and the scarcity of some luxuries. They remarked that it's funny that when things were plentiful that no one wanted them, but now that they're scarce they were missed. In the Harbour Bar four friends met to quench their thirst, two of them with red lemonade and the others with pints of Guinness, before going to join their ship in Cardiff port. They talked about the vessel, the City of Waterford, and the other shipmates that they'd soon be joining. There'd be no shortage of company on their voyage as the ship was a small one yet carried a crew of 23. The four sat on stools against the stained mahogany counter, J. P. Lennon of Sidmonton Avenue, Bray, was chief officer; beside him was John Ryan of Dock Terrace, where the Harbour Bar is, who was bosun; next was J. Bowden and Sam Naylor, both also of Dock Terrace. They finished their drinks, said goodbye to the landlord, slung

Bray from the sea

their bags over their shoulders and made their way to Bray station, just around the corner, where they caught the steam train for Dublin.

It was a very dark night on September 18-19th. The sea was dead calm and not a sound was heard except the steady rhythm of the engine and the faint hiss of the ship cutting steadily through the water. On the bridge of the City of Waterford was the watch, comprising an officer and helmsman. It would soon be dawn. Both men were tired and looking forward to being relieved, so that they could go to their bunks. Already the familiar sounds of an awakening ship could be heard, the rattle and clang of cooking utensils in the galley, the banging of an occasional door and the clunk of heavy boots on an iron deck. The sun's rays would soon illuminate the Saorstat and Continental Steam Shipping Company's old veteran and pride, the City of Waterford, which was travelling for safety in convoy.

Dawn had broken two hours ago and it was now 7.30 and all ships in the group could be seen travelling closely together, with them was a Dutch tug which found difficulty in keeping its position. John Ryan of Bray had just come up on deck when the tug collided with the City of Waterford. The impact was of such strength that the crew below thought that they had been torpedoed.

The ship commenced to list badly to starboard and then fell to port. All the crew were immediately on deck and, as the situation appeared hopeless, the order to abandon ship was given by Captain Alpin of Monkstown in Dublin. They launched two lifeboats, one was commanded by Alpin and the other by Chief

Officer Lennon of Bray. All the crew were well and accounted for. Some twenty minutes later they watched, with great sadness, their ship sink to the ocean's bed.

The cold and miserable crew were soon picked up by a small rescue craft and within a short time they were transferred to a larger vessel, the Walmer Castle, built in Belfast a few short years before, which was luxurious compared with the City of Waterford, which had been sailing for thirty six years.

The following day, Saturday, September 20th, a wolf pack found the convoy. The torpedoes started to hit their targets and the ships started to go down. The Walmer Castle managed to rescue many of the badly-wounded sailors, and soon her decks and accommodation were filled with the survivors. The Waterford's crew helped give aid to the wounded.

Next day, Sunday 21st, shortly after noon, all was quiet except for the cries of the wounded and the dying, the horizon was clear. Bowden of Bray was on the deck with another two of his rescued comrades when he saw, with great horror, a dive bomber coming in low over the water on the port side. He watched helplessly as two bombs were dropped, one exploding amidships and the other a direct hit forward. Nearly all those on deck were killed instantly; among them were three members of the Waterford's crew. Captain Alpin, Edward Kearney of Marino in Dublin and Sam Naylor of Bray never knew what happened. Pat Murphy of Dunlaoghaire and George Furlong (second engineer) lay dying. Chief Engineer Williams, James Brown, M.C. Ryan and Chief Officer J.P. Lennon of Bray were badly injured. What tragedy, what cruel fate ! Who said that lightning never struck twice in the same place.

A raft was lowered from the sinking ship and the wounded and other survivors from the Waterford placed on it. This raft was attached to the mortally-wounded vessel by a strong three-inch rope, and those on it realised too late that they hadn't any knife. It appeared that they were going to be pulled down by the rapidly disappearing Walmer Castle as it sank below the waves. One of those left on the stricken rescue vessel, which would soon become his tomb, threw a small ladies penknife to the raft where it was caught by one of the Waterford's crew. They managed to saw through the strong hemp just in time, before the ship disappeared under the hungry sea forever.

What were the thoughts that went through the poor survivors consciousness as they floated about? Wet, cold, exhausted, skin stinging and raw from the saltwater, miserable and helpless; forgive us our trespasses; unsure whether to pray for rescue again or a release from the present agony of living; never-ending peace; the comfort of God's presence forever; will we be plucked from

96

the sea again only to prolong the appalling agony? "Don't nod off or the gulls will take our eyes", Bray Harbour, the Promenade and the warm comfort of the Harbour Bar on a cold winter's evening. 'Thy will be done'.

Once again they were rescued from a dreadful death. Chief Engineer Williams and James Brown were put into hospital in Liverpool and Chief Officer Lennon from Bray with Ryan from Amiens Street were hospitalised in Gibraltar. Second Engineer Furlong from Wexford and Pat Murphy from Dunlaoghaire died on the rescue ship, comforted by the tears and prayers of their surviving shipmates. They were on a total of seven battle scarred-vessels since their ship went down. A few thoughts keep running through my mind. Why didn't the families of these men and others who met a similar fate receive pensions? Surely they sacrificed their lives for their country? Or is this reward reserved for those who carry guns, kill or wear a uniform?

Down the Quinsboro Road, beside the Legion of Mary's premises next to the level crossing and opposite to where the International Hotel once stood, there is a large memorial cross to those who fell in the 1914 -18 war, the one to end all wars! There is not one name of any member of the merchant navy, British or Irish, on this. Was their death worth less, or was it that the dead from Bray who are to be remembered must have worn a crown on a badge? Sam, no one wears a poppy for you. You are far beyond these human thoughts that stem from the bitterness of human frailty. You can never again be hurt as you dwell in the light of God's presence forever!

GREYSTONES

The first known reference to this delightful town occurs in a map of Wicklow dated 1760 and names 'Gray Stones'. In 1795 it was described as:

a noted fishing place 4 miles beyond Bray and 14 from Dublin. The herrings first brought into Dublin are usually taken by fishing boats of this place.

The surveyor, Robert Fraser, in 1800 wrote :

at Gray Stones I found a rock stretching out into the sea and forming a fine natural harbour. adjacent to this harbour is a plain which might be formed into a convenient village, into which fishermen scattered on the coast might with advantage be collected and by having some improvement made of this harbour, they would not be exposed to the losses to which they are so frequently subjected but is the occasion of numbers annually perishing.

In the Parliamentary Gazetteer of 1845 the description is very comprehensive:

GREYSTONES, a headland, and a fishing village, 3 miles south by east of Bray, half barony of Rathdown, Co. Wicklow, Leinster. The headland is a small and bleak projection, consisting of hard slate rock and constituting the only object of interest over a distance of several miles on the coast road from Bray; and it extends about 365 feet from the beach, and has for the most part, at its base, from 12 to 14 feet of water at the ebb of spring tides. A quay and a breakwater on the north side of the headland were planned by Mr. Nimmo, at an estimated expense of £3,424.12.3; but though a public grant of £461.10.9 was made in aid of its execution, it has not, we believe, been adopted. A great number of row boats employed in the fisheries must here be hauled on shore when the wind blows from any point between north and east north east. Though the inhabitants of the village itself are only a coastguard party and the families of 5 or 6 fishermen, the number of fishing craft belonging to the place amounts to about 3 half-decked vessels with 18 men, and 31 open sail boats with 186 men. Greystones is on the estate of Mr. La Touche.

All the references stressed the need of a substantial harbour and because this was not constructed many lives were lost over the years. The small village was soon to change its character from a poor fishing community through events over which the inhabitants had no control. Fishing would no longer be a priority. A new world began for them in 1856. The railway had arrived! Their dependence changed from the harvest of the sea to the attraction of the wealthy from the land to the beauty of their coastline and magnificent beaches. When Bray station opened in 1854 the engineers and workmen looked towards Bray Head and perceived an insurmountable obstacle, they thought that they'd come to the end of the line. Permission to build the rail inland, around the Head, was refused by the Earl of Meath. The situation appeared hopeless until the great engineer Isambard Kingdom Brunel (1806-1859), who was celebrated for his work on the Menai Bridge in Wales and the Thames Tunnel in London, was asked to help. It was he who was responsible for building the single line and blasting the way through Bray Head so that the Greystones and Delgany station was opened in 1856. Brunel's tunnels here are sometimes referred to as 'Brunel's Folly' as they were subjected to coastal erosion and rockfalls. The line had subsequently to be moved a few yards further inland.

Greystones was now easily reached from Dublin, and for the first time people could visit on daily excursions and soon it became a fashionable resort like Bray. With the increasing numbers coming to live there it was soon necessary to build a church, so in 1864 with the help of £4,000 from Peter La Touche, Saint Patrick's (Church of Ireland) on Church Road was consecrated. Numbers continued to grow and the church had to be extended to accommodate the congregation in 1875, again in 1888 and 1898. Large houses were built on Church Road and Trafalgar Road between 1864 and 1889. The foundation stone for the Presbyterian church was laid in June 1887. And how did this population explosion affect the Catholics in the area? It didn't, because they were few in number. Out of a total population of 500 in 1891, there were only four Catholics residing in the town. At Blacklion, on the outskirts, there is a church, St. Killian's, built in 1866 for the people in outlying areas working on the farms. Their numbers soon increased, many being summer visitors, and in 1895 a site of one acre was obtained for a ground rent of £25 per annum and an iron prefab building was erected at a cost of £405, which included a bell. A curate's house was built at the same time for £700. Dr. Donnelly, parish priest of Bray sent Father Luby, the first curate, to Greystones. Father Tom Hill succeeded Father Luby in 1899 when he was transferred to Dublin. The iron chapel was destroyed in a storm in 1905; subsequently the stone church of the Holy Rosary was built when Father Timothy Gorman was PP of Bray and Greystones. Within this church can be seen two magnificent stained-glass windows by that great Irish artist, Evie Hone.

The town's new livelihood was now that of tourism as it had become a famous and favourite 'watering spot' for upper and middle-class holiday makers. A typical advertisement from this early period reads:

It is a well sheltered winter residence, standing in its own specially laid out grounds; containing neatly arranged lawns for tennis, croquet and etc.; and adjacent to excellent golf links. And a special feature of this hotel is the select class of ladies and gentlemen who frequent it all the year round. All the appointments are up-to-date. Terms from 2 to 3 guineas a week according to season and position of bedroom.

Another description, in 1912, was :

The great charm of Greystones consists of its unconveniality and the absence of the features which go to make up the typical watering place, while its golf links, its picturesque surroundings, and the pleasing combinations of rural and seaside scenery in its neighbourhood, combine to render it a most attractive and restful holiday resort.

Among the oldest names in Greystones are Archer, Evans, who built the first slate-roofed house here, and Spurling, who have been long associated with the sea. These families have been responsible for rescuing many sailors from a watery grave through their volunteer work with the Coast Life Saving Service. I'll tell you a bit more about this in the next chapter. Greystones is now a large and thriving town, but retains much of the unique and intimate character associated with its polite past. Long may it continue to please the visitors who arrive and enjoy its many splendid attractions, among which are the comforts that the Beach House and the La Touche Hotel have to offer the weary traveller.

THE LAST ROCKET RESCUE AT BRAY

A coast life-saving service was established in Greystones in the nineteenth century under the British government, and when independence for the twenty-six counties was won in 1922, this service was taken over and continued by the Department of Industry and Commerce in the newly established Irish Free State. All the volunteers who had previously enrolled under the British Board of Trade re-enrolled under the Irish government without any exceptions. Most had joined the service in their early twenties and many served in the station for over forty years. The details of those members are as follows:

Name	Date of Birth	Year of enrolment	Residence	Distance from station
Osborne Spurling	1858	1887	Laburnum Cottage	100 yards
James Darcy	1879	1901	Grove Cottage	1/2 mile
George Archer	1881	1902	Burlington House	200 yards
James Lawless	1865	1886	Greystones	200 yards
William Spurling	1888	1910	Laburnum Cottage	100 yards
Charles Evans	1866	1886	Seaview House	300 yards
Edmond Evans	1883	1903	Norman Lodge	300 yards
Michael Keddy	1878	1903	Strand Cottage	400 yards
Edward Archer	1865	1886	Burlington House	200 yards
John Spurling	1890	1913	Laburnum Cottage	100 yards
Andrew Martin	1862	1886	Greystones	1/4 mile
Michael Whiston	1869	1901	Strand Cottage	500 yards
John Evans	1862	1890	Sweet Briar Cottage	150 yards
Albert Archer	1888	1912	Kenmare Cottage	100 yards
Henry Evans	1878	1916	Eden Cottage	150 yards

Osborne Spurling, James Lawless, Charles Evans, Edward Archer and Andrew Archer were awarded coveted and distinguished long-service medals. The number one man in charge was Osborne Spurling and his son, William, became number two. The inspector of the station was Tom Casement, who was so proud of his patriot brother Roger, that he wouldn't permit his name to be spoken in a public house. Both went to school in Bray.

Inspections and drill-exercises were held every three or four months under the critical eye of the inspector, who commended the men for their speed and efficiency. His remarks, entered in the station's log-book, read for the most part "drill very good 10 minutes" and "drill v. good as usual, rocket fired 9 minutes".

The variety of stores in stock was immense and varied; the list included over 150 essential items, all most necessary for the saving of life at sea. The most important items were the rockets and flares, of which there was a total of thirty eight. With the help of these, the volunteers were able to get a line on to a vessel and effect a rescue with a breeches buoy. This was done by firing a large rocket to which was attached a light line. The line would be taken by the boat's crew that were in peril, and then they would take in a heavier line which was attached to the light one. This heavy line enabled a harness (breeches buoy) to be pulled aboard and each man would take turns to be pulled ashore by their rescuers.

It was a dreadful night, on January 30th 1926, when force eight gales created havoc with shipping in the Irish Sea. The driving force of the sleet and the rain, in freezing temperatures, stung the faces of the poor sailors like so many needles. All through the following day the storm raged and lashed the coast. It was impossible to walk Bray Promenade without being consumed by the ever-hungry sea. The south-east wind screeched and howled like a thousand banshees. It was a fisherman in one of the small cottages in Dock Terrace, just beside the Harbour Bar, who saw a small ketch aground just north of the estuary. It was most fortunate that the vessel was noticed, as night had fallen quickly and it was soon as dark as the devil's soul. Word was sent by telephone at 18.45 p.m., to Greystones, where the alarm was raised at the watch station by one of the volunteers on duty who immediately sent up a maroon flare to summon the rest of the service, who were at prayer in church. The equipment wagon left the rocket house, when all the crew were assembled, at 19.15 and departed for Bray, arriving there at 20.20, when the gear was immediately set up. At 20.30 the rocket had been fired and contact made with the stricken vessel. The crew of the Marie Celine, nearly two days out of Drogheda, were lifted ashore by breeches buoy and comforted by all those present on the harbour wall beneath the lighthouse, long after blown into the sea by another fierce storm. The wretched survivors were most pitiful to behold and Mr. Spurling, who was in charge of the whole operation, asked the superintendent of the Civic Guards, who were present, to open the Harbour Bar's facilities for the brave assembly. The super informed them that he hadn't the authority to open a licensed premises as it was against the law, it being after hours. Spurling, in a loud and imperious voice exclaimed "I have the authority and I'm ordering you to have the facilities of the famous hostelry placed at our disposal. I'm giving you carte blanche to open the premises!" The doors were soon unlocked and the steadily growing multitude were comfortably installed inside. The rescued and rescuers were soon warmed and cheered by the quality and quantity of the liquid refreshment and nourishment provided. The hospitality and sustenance continued until dawn of the next day, February 1st.

This heroic rescue, nearly three quarters of a century ago, was the last time that a rescue rocket and breeches buoy was used in Bray. It is interesting to record that whenever Mr. Spurling's thirst had cause to make him enter the Harbour Bar after this famous episode, his moderate inclination was quenched free-of-charge by both the landlord and admiring customers. The Harbour Bar to-day is run by Paul and Des O'Toole, and Captain Neville Spurling, the son of our famous hero, visits it occasionally on a Saturday afternoon, but regrettably has to pay hard cash for his refreshment.

The Coastal Life Saving Service that continued until after the foundation of our infant state now no longer exists.

THE FEVER

A word that would strike fear into the population in those Victorian times. You see, it was not only hunger that was responsible for so many deaths in Ireland during that period. Death came in another and perhaps more fearsome guise, and was no respecter of class or circumstance, a death from which there was little chance of escape, even for those whose appetites were always satisfied. A word that struck terror and despair into our community, CHOLERA, it was to stalk the land laying its cold hand on many and leading them to their graves in the prime of their lives.

Bray wasn't to escape the terrible disease that was to present an appalling spectacle of misery and sorrow by the continuous flow of sad funeral processions to St. Peter's, St. Paul's, Old Connacht and Kilmacanogue cemeteries throughout many decades of the nineteenth century. At the same time typhoid was rampant and was confused with cholera, but to most of Bray's population there was no difference, they described the scourge of the grim reaper as simply, 'the fever'. The spread of the contagion was swift because of the condition in which the people had to live. Contemporary medical notes read:

> *The great want of house accommodation for the lower classes is a formidable obstruction to sanitary measures. The damp state of the weather is favourable to the development of the scourge.*

Poor peoples lives at the time were cheap and there was little pity or sympathy from authority for the bereaved. Medical advice at the time on how to combat the disease read:

> *As the great depression of the vital powers and the consequent coldness of the surface it is obvious that to rouse the system and restore the warmth of the surface of the body are the objects that require to be effected. A vapour or hot air bath should be had recourse to if at hand, as this, however, will probably but seldom be the case, put the patient into a hot bed and apply a large hot mustard poultice over the pit of the stomach. Then let a blanket wrung out of a tub full of boiling water, as hot and dry as possible, be laid over his body. Put bottles of hot water, bags of hot sand or hot bricks or tiles wrapped in flannel into the bed.*

This advice ends with the consoling words "Do not fear catching the complaint yourself. Your very exertions will be the best and surest means of preventing your being attacked." Alas, these cures and assurances were of no benefit to one of the most prominent of Bray's doctors who helped combat the spread of infection; he himself caught the fever from his patients and his memorial in front of the Royal Hotel reads:

This Fountain Is Erected
To The Memory Of
Christopher Thompson
FFCSI
Who Died Dec. 16. 1876
In Testimony Of His Worth

Dr. Thompson's remains lie just across the road in St. Paul's churchyard with many of his patients.

It was the sanitary conditions that prevailed that caused the spread of the disease; and Bray was in an appalling condition in the nineteenth century because of lack of toilets, sewers and the un-hygienic disposal of waste. It was a veritable breeding ground for 'the fever'. The Urban Sanitary Authority of Bray was established to combat the causes, and they were given power to have houses levelled if they found it necessary. Many of the small cottages were rented and it was the landlords who were responsible for the awful state in which the poor had to live. Here are some samples taken from their minute book:

Friday Nov. 27th. 1874 : The Sanitary Officer's (Dr. Whistler's) reports were read. Report of Nov. 13th. relative to sickness in a house occupied by Hickey on Wicklow Road. also no privy. Ordered that the Sub Sanitary Officer serve notice to provide a privy; Nov. 18th. relative to the sewage connected with Vevay House and the Old Court School as also the privies of the latter. Ordered that the Sub Sanitary Officer serve the proper notices on the Earl of Meath or his agent and also Mr. Martin of Vevay House to have those complaints remedied; Nov. 23rd. Report of 38 houses in Hudsons Terrace without privies or ashpits and sewerage defective.; Nov. 23rd. 38 Houses in Purcells Field. 4 houses in Matthews Lane (Little Bray), 7 Houses in Doyles Field (Great Bray), 17 Houses in Pound Lane, 9 houses in Cliftons Lane (L.B), all the houses in Back Street.; 4th March 1875. 6 houses in Mill Lane the property of Mrs. Collins unhealthy condition without yards, privies or sewers. All houses in Pound Lane not fit for habitation. Notice to be served on the owner and occupiers that if they are not left the premises within one month, they not being fit for human habitation, they will be summoned. ; 12th April. 4 houses on the strand, occupied by Thomas Byrne, Eliza Clair, John Carty and John Devitt, without yards, privies or sewers. 6 houses on the Dargle Road, the property of Mr. Gibson. 6 houses in Church Terrace, the property of Lord Pembroke.; 15th November . A letter from Mr. Tennett was read stating that the houses in Pound Lane will be levelled in a few days; July 8th 1878. A report from Dr. Whistler as to his having prevented, assisted by A. Geagan, a convalescent case of smallpox being brought into the town was read; 10th March 1879. On the recommendation of Dr. Whistler it was ordered to provide clothes for the nurse (Cullen) who attended Allen in smallpox and have her present clothes destroyed. The cost of the new clothes not to exceed two pounds.

The litany in the minute book is unending. Dr. Whistler is also buried in St. Paul's with Dr. Thompson.

All this has, thankfully, changed today and our Bray Urban District Council, together with the many doctors who dwell here, ensure that we live in a clean and healthy environment. Great improvements have taken place since the turn of the nineteenth century because of our laws, not least of which is that which governs the sale and descriptions of medicines. Around the time of 'the fever', and before that, there were patent medicines and remedies that were advertised, boasting of miracle cures; yet there were no controls for that sort of thing. Quacks thrived. Let me tell you about that time.

MID 19th CENTURY CURES

When the time of year arrives, when the cold weather appears to be behind us and we look forward to a few warm summer months, most of us have experienced flu, coughs and sneezes which we have thankfully recovered from. That is the time to build up a resistance to the germus malignus that will surely assail us again when the cold weather returns once more. A proper diet will supply us with the necessary vitamins that are required to combat the usual common cold and flu, and our local chemist shops have a large variety of medicines which can be trusted to cure most ailments, provided that the recommended professional advice for their application or consumption is obeyed. But what did the people of Bray do around the 1840s and before that?

Two hundred years ago there were 'apothecaries' who sold drugs and who were partially-trained in medicine, before them there were barbers who, as well as giving you a close shave and haircut, would bleed you to relieve blood pressure or any other ailment that you thought you had. The barber also carried around a jar of leeches (remember Humphery Bogart in The African Queen!) which when applied to the skin, gorged themselves on your blood, when their appetite was satiated they were withdrawn and placed back in the jar where they lived to be available for the next patient. And so the barbers were surgeons and the apothecaries were doctors until the world got a bit older and people wiser, more skilled and educated in the treatment of illnesses.

In Bray, around the 1840s, the chemist shops sold an assortment of the most curious medicines and, if their curative boasts were to be true, it's a wonder that anyone ever died. The following is a small selection of what was available:

Mr. Cockles Pills for Indigestion, Liver Complaints etc.
What's rank, or title, station, state , or wealth
To that far greater worldly blessing, health ?
What's house or land or dress or wine or meat,
If one can't get rest for pain nor sleep nor eat.

Moxon's Effervescent Magnesian Aperient.
It is of eminent service in pains of the head,
bilious infections, nausea, sickness, heartburn,
indigestion, gout and piles.

Spencer's pulmonic Elixir.
a certain and speedy cure for coughs, colds asthma, influenza, incipient consumption and all disorders of the chest and lungs.

Powell's Balsam of Anniseed.

for coughs, shortness of breath, asthmas etc. Under the immediate patronage of several of the most distinguished nobility and gentry in the Kingdom. Testimony of several of the most eminent members of the medical profession who, with great liberality, recommended it as a family cough medicine, renders any eulogism on the part of the proprietor unnecessary.

Mr. Thomas's Succendaneum

for stopping decayed teeth. Patronised by Her Majesty, His Royal Highness Prince Albert and her Royal Highness the Duchess of Kent.

Rowland's Kalydor.

Under the special patronage of Her Most Gracious Majesty the Queen and the Royal Family- eradicates all pimples, spots, redness, tan freckles and other defects of the skin.

Perhaps the greatest boast at the time, even surpassing miracles, was the strangest medicine of them all:

Compound Decoction of Sarsaparilla.

A sure cure for scurvy, eruptions of the face, chronic rheumatism, chronic liver affections, the effects of taking mercury. Sold in bottles 4s 6p (equal to 6 pints of the decoction).

Life hasn't changed so much that the petty vanities that assail us now were any different then. Growing old gracefully was never accepted especially when it came to baldness. How on earth did their hair fall out when they had the following certain remedies:

Baldness Removed and Prevented.

The Pomade Depurative. Invented by a Physician of the highest celebrity, Will in all instances restore the hair so long as vitality remains in the bud from which it springs.

Ashley's Anti-Depilatory Extract.

Warranted to stop the hair falling out; also to free the head immediately from scurf.

Castor Oil Pomatum.

Kett's highly perfumed castor oil for beautifying the hair will stand pre-eminent for promoting its growth and giving it a glossy appearance.

In those far off days there was no Advertising Code of Standards - and no insurance to be claimed in court if the medicines failed to act or act in an adverse manner. Retiring in the evening with a full head of hair and awakening totally bald was sometimes recorded. (There was an incident of a person taking a cure and within three days becoming striped like a zebra!).

Of course, all this was before eminent chemists and pharmacists were established in Bray like A.L Doran of 1 Goldsmith's Terrace, Mackey's of 21 Florence Road, Raverty's Medical Hall of 110 Main Street and James Vance of 92 Main Street, which was changed to Vance and Wilson and cared for by the O'Brien Brothers. There were no cures for the dreadful hunger of 1846 to 1850; let me try and describe to you what life was like then.

1845

In 1995 there was a spate of articles in our national newspapers which gave the impression that that year was the 150th anniversary of the Famine. Such writings were incorrect; that year didn't see any famine in Ireland because the potato crop of 1844 fed the people in 1845 and the blight which destroyed the vegetable in 1845 did not have such catastrophic consequences until 1846. There was 'hunger' from 1846 to 1849, yet there was sufficient food to feed the people three times over, but they couldn't afford to buy it and so they starved.

What was Bray like then? The railway hadn't yet arrived here and therefore the grand Victorian edifices had not yet been built. The courthouse had just been recently opened (1841), and there were some well built houses on Main Street, with a large number of small thatched cottages in Little Bray, where most of the population dwelt. The big buildings standing then were St. Paul's, the Catholic 'Chapel' (later to be enlarged and be called a 'church' dedicated to Most Holy Redeemer), Mr. Quin's hotel, St Peter's, the Barracks and The Maltings.

Ireland had experienced many periods of famine and pestilence down through its turbulent history – but the population in those times was small and communication methods with the outside world slow, so that assistance to alleviate the suffering was never forthcoming.

By 1845 vast changes had occurred. Newspapers thrived in Great Britain and Ireland, and people were well-acquainted with what was happening here and throughout the world. Railways were developing, regular sailing routes were established, and a new era of rapid communication was being born.

The staple diet of the people was the humble potato, which possessed such wondrous nutritional properties that the population had increased and multiplied, and they were strong and healthy. Reports coming from Ireland during that fateful year, the eve of the appalling catastrophe, were varied:

Jan 1st. 1845 : Chapter of the Order of St. Patrick

The Lord Lieutenant, as Grand Master of the Most Illustrious Order of St. Patrick, held a chapter on Saturday at Dublin Castle, when the Earl of Rosse and the Marquis of Waterford, having received the honour of knighthood, were admitted as knights of the order with the usual formalities. The Primate, Lord John Beresford, read the declaration, which was subscribed by the new knights. During the investiture the Lord Primate sat and stood alternately on the right of his Excellency the Grand Master, and on his left was placed his Grace the Archbishop of Dublin. The knights present were :- the Earl of Meath, the Earl of Roden, the Earl of Claremont, the Earl of Donoughmore, the Marquis of Headford, the Earl of Milltown and the Earl of Wicklow.

March 29th: The Banquet to Mr. O'Connell at Kilkenny.

The long talked of banquet to Mr. O'Connell and the other 'Repeal Martyrs' took place at Kilkenny on Tuesday. The procession was an immense one. By some, the numbers of Repealers was estimated at 30,000. On Mr. O'Connell's carriage were the principal martyr, Mr. John O'Connell, Mr. Barrett, Mr. Steele, Mr. Ray and Mr. Smith O'Brien.

April 12th: The Queen's Visit to Ireland.

The Royal Visit has become the universal topic in Ireland. It is generally supposed that Her Majesty and her illustrious Consort will arrive about the middle of July. It is stated that plans of the apartments in Dublin Castle, and in the Vice Regal Lodge, Phoenix Park, have been taken by her Majesty's desire and forwarded to Buckingham Palace.

April 12th: More Wonders of the Electric Telegraph.

The division upon the Maynooth grant, which took place in the House of Commons on Saturday morning last, at three o'clock, was known and printed at Southampton by half past three, by means of the electric telegraph.

Oct. 18th: Irish Railways. New Irish Railway Projects.

A company is in progress of formation in Dublin, to be entitled the 'Dublin Southern Villa Railway Company', for the purpose of constructing a line of railway from Dublin to Rathfarnham and Ballyboden, with branches to Tallaght on one side, and on the other to Milltown, Dundrum, and through the Vale of Shangannah, to join the Bray line.

But most of the reports being published were of a disturbing character, unrest and extreme dissatisfaction was the normal news of the day.

July 5th: Disturbed State of Part of Ireland
House of Commons, Monday.

In answer to some questions from Sir E. Hayes respecting the system of intimidation and murder, Sir James Graham stated that the Government felt the greatest anxiety respecting the outrages and crime and that every possible means had been taken to suppress them. The military and the police forces have been recently increased in those counties.

That year also witnessed the death of Thomas Davis :

Sept. 20th.: Death of a Member of the Repeal Association.

Mr. Davis, the principal contributor to the Nation newspaper, and the acknowledged leader of the Young Ireland party, died at an early hour on Tuesday morning. His death was very unexpected, and will be greatly lamented, particularly by all who were connected with him in politics. He died of malignant typhus fever.

And what did the papers report about the potato?

October 11th: The Potato Disease.

Accounts received from different parts of Ireland show that the disease in the potato crop is extending far and wide, and causing great alarm amongst the peasantry. The Belfast Newsletter has still a more lamentable account. It says 'we have abstained from occupying our space with the accounts of the prevalence of this calamity in various places, for this reason, that there is hardly a district in Ireland in which the potato crops at present are uninfected - perhaps we might say, hardly a field.'

December: Mr. Daniel O'Connell reports:

One third of the potato crop was destroyed and none could tell how much further the disease would go. The fever follows scarcity. This is invariably the case. In Waterford, Wexford, Drogheda and Kerry fever was awfully prevalent. The agricultural labourers were on the verge of starvation. The rate of wage for labourers was one shilling and six pence a week. There were differences of opinion as to when the famine would commence, for his part he thought it would commence as early as January.

And so , as the year drew to a close it became apparent that Ireland's pitiful fate was sealed and that it would become one vast charnel house, the field beside Rathdown Union in Loughlinstown would soon be filled with the unmarked graves of the poor.

CHRISTMAS IN BRAY

When it came to Christmas that year, the people in Bray, and throughout the rest of Ireland did celebrate the occasion, although they were on the verge of the dreadful starvation that was to wipe out one million of them and force a further million to flee their native land within the next four years. Most were unaware of the seriousness of the situation and, therefore, the appalling calamity that was imminent was not to the fore in their conversation. What was Bray like then? The geography of the town hasn't changed greatly, except for the fact that there was no Town Hall as we know it, and many of the houses were much smaller and had thatched roofs. There was no railway and many streets that we have now weren't there. But if someone from that period were to time-travel back (a Rip Van Winkle so to speak) they'd have no difficulty in recognising where they were. Little Bray was a thriving community and St. Peter's Church, with Father Harold, was not long opened, further up on Main Street there was St. Paul's and the big Catholic Church behind three houses. The architecture was much simpler, Victoria had not long been on the throne, so that big and imposing Victorian type edifices were yet to arrive.

Can you imagine what the festive season was like then? No piped water, no electricity which meant no TV no 'Wizard of Oz' or 'Willy Wonka's Chocolate Factory'!, no phones, artificial light, gas or electric cookers, no plastic, no piped music, no jingle bells. Well, maybe we wouldn't survive today, but then the people coped allright, and managed to enjoy and be grateful for what they had.

The residents and visitors in Mr. Quin's hotel were reading the newspapers of that Christmas week, and the main item they discussed was what was described as 'The Ministerial Crisis'. This was because John Russell of the Whigs (Liberals) had been unable to form a government and the famine Queen, Victoria, summoned Robert Peel out of retirement to form a Tory one. All this was very confusing and complicated but was mostly due to differences of opinion about the Corn Laws. Basically, these were laws in operation which protected the affluent farmers and landowners by imposing duty on imported corn, so that the price of the home product was kept at a very high level. The hotel was a thriving establishment filled with shining lights from the numerous candles and lanterns, and large open fires to keep the regular patrons and travellers warm. The customers pockets clinked and jingled with coins. The aromas of the succulent dishes cooking in the kitchens wafted into the street outside, where the delicious scents were savoured by some of the poor who were gathered around the entrance.

While the patrons politely balanced their fragile china teacups, or their little twinkling glasses of port or sherry, they read what the 'Liberator', Daniel O'Connell, had said that week. He was ready to support Peel in any good measure that he proposed for Ireland, whether to repeal the Corn Laws or reduce the price of food to avert the impending famine. He cared neither for Whigs or Tories and he would vote for any proposal, no matter who brought it forward, if it was a good one.

They had purchased their presents, some of which were advertised in the papers:

> *Musical Presents:- Little songs for Little Singers, Nursery Songs, and Little Vocal Duets, Indian Melodies, Canadian Airs, Psalms of the Church" or " The Comic Annual for 1846: Now ready, price of only 12s bound. An amusing Christmas and New Year gift" or " Acceptable Presents:- The present season is hallowed by one of the most delightful offices of Friendship and Affection; the interchange of gifts as remembrances of the donors, and tokens of their esteem for the receivers. To combine these requisites a more fitting souvenir cannot be suggested than Rowland's Toilet Articles, the Macassar Oil, Kalydor and Odonto, each of infallible attributes* and so on.*

Children of the average family had no toys, perhaps a wooden spinning top or a hoop made by their father or relation. A good doll cost two months wages for an average labouring man; nevertheless, the children had their pleasures in the games that they played and in their fertile imagination, which kept them dreaming of a better future.

And what other entertainment was there? Well there were stories exchanged around the fireside, with the light of the flickering flames shining on all the faces. Stories of pucas, banshees and of Christmases long ago. Stories and news that were filtering through to Bray from Dublin and London. Tidings that kept all those listening amazed and enthralled in wonderment. They all sang the songs made popular by Mr. Tom Moore whose fame had spread across the seas, 'The Minstrel Boy' and 'The Harp That Once'. They discussed the recent trials held in the newly built courthouse beside the bridge over the Dargle, and the severity of the sentences handed out by the majesty of the law. Liquid refreshment was mostly of the alcoholic kind. Father Matthew's temperance campaign was at it's height. The unfortunate people had to bear much hardship, so it wasn't a bit surprising that they 'fell by the wayside' and recommenced to imbibe strong spirituous beverages, which cost very little at the time, to help them forget their troubles until the next day. Poitin was readily available in the town, but the wealthy could indulge in Government whiskey and fine wines.

Some homes had reason to celebrate other events as well as Christmas. Recent births were Matthew Kinsella, Thomas Byrne (whose mother's maiden name was Gaskin), Sarah Kinsella, Edward Mc Cabe (mother's maiden name Mary Glynn) Mary Hackman and Mary Keane (mother's name Essy Connor). Marriages close to Christmas were between Francis Murray and Judith Roche, Jacob Kavanagh and Mary Ryan, Hugh Bolger and Elizabeth Byrne. Some children celebrating their first birthday were Christopher Synott, Elizabeth Byrne, Elizabeth Deveraux, Edward Murphy and Thomas Murphy.

And it was then that the tradition of Christmas Trees, outside of Germany, began to become fashionable. They were described as:

> *This is the usual mode of celebrating the Eve of the birth of Christ, in Germany. In almost every family, is set up this pleasing figure, having the resemblance of a growing tree, loaded with a profusion of fruits and flowers; and upon its branches, the different members of the family suspend the little presents which they intend for those they love best; and on the exhibition of the tree, the presents are claimed by the donors, and handed, with compliments, to their friends.*

They wondered at the great changes that were occurring in the modern times that they were living in and read the following mind boggling piece of information:

> *A lady breakfasted at Edinburgh on Monday morning, and arrived at Sligo next afternoon, 66 miles by land, and 240 by sea, in 26 hours!*

Just as we do today, they 'small talked' about the weather. This report was in the newspaper:

> *During the last five or six days we have had every variety of weather-almost summer mildness, heavy gales of wind from the north west, west and south west, fog, copious downpourings of rain, hail, snow, sharp frost, quickly succeeded by more rain, and a temperature exceeding 45 degrees. On Saturday and Sunday the gale was terrific, accompanied by rain, hail and blinding snow gusts. On Sunday, the snow, in places lay on the ground five inches in depth. On Tuesday morning, the ice, in exposed situations, was nearly half an inch in thickness at daylight, but by nine o'clock the frost gave way and more rain and snow fell. Wednesday (Christmas Eve) was a fine seasonable day.*

The shops were filled with geese, and turkeys had just become popular; it was only the very wealthy that could afford these, as the prices were far beyond the means of the ordinary working person. Prices of turkeys were from 3/- to 25/-; geese from 3/6 to 12/-; fowls from 2/6 to 10/6 per pair; hares from 2/6 to 5/- each . In to-day's values that's like saying the cost of your Christmas dinner is from one to two weeks wages! The fowl were hung from poles outside the butchers, you can still see how it was done if you inspect Frank Doyle's shop, formerly Dempsey Brothers, on our congested Main Street. They hung in hundreds, sometimes from the outside windows over the shops. The poor, as were most of the population, through scrimping and some small saving throughout the year, perhaps could afford to buy an old hen for the table and maybe a piece of bacon. You might imagine that a duck or a rabbit was available, but to have such game would indicate that they had been procured by poaching and there were severe penalties imposed on those found in possession of them. The main dish was the humble potato, which was cooked in a variety of ways and the more fortunate might be treated to dumplings made from stale bread and suet.   I remember, from my childhood, a little poem which might have come from that time:

> *Christmas is coming and the goose is getting fat*
> *Please put a penny in the poor man's hat,*
> *If you haven't got a penny a ha'penny will do,*
> *If you haven't got a ha'penny a piece of bread will do,*
> *If you haven't got a piece of bread then God bless you.*

It was only the very rich that could afford plum pudding. These days we hear more and more people saying "it gets earlier each year!" and "there's too much commercialism about it!". Nowadays we are inclined to believe that expense, waste and gluttony at Christmas is a newly-arrived modern state of affairs. We are wrong! In those far off days, long past, there was great emphasis on eating and drinking, even the words of Christmas carols left a lot to be desired in those long forgotten days before Christmas became Xmas and St. Stephen's Day became Boxing Day. Here's a carol or song that was popular then:

> *A loud and laughing welcome to the merry Christmas bells,*
> *All hail with happy gladness to the well-known chant that swells,*
> *We list' the pealing anthem chord, we hear the midnight strain,*
> *And love the tidings that proclaim old Christmas time again,*
> *But there must be a melody of purer deeper sound,*
> *A rich keynote, whose chorus runs through all the music round,*
> *Let kindly voices ring beneath low roof or palace dome,*
> *For those alone are carol chimes that bless a Christmas home.*

Of course, in Bray they realised what Christmas was really all about. That it was a time to enjoy, and also to celebrate the birth of their Saviour nearly two thousand years before. The wonder of Christmas then was the same as it is today; the great feeling of contentment and happiness at the awesome mystery of Christ's humble birth in a stable, which was narrated again to everyone at religious services. So you see, without any television, tinsel decorations, flashing lights, luxurious and exotic foods, expensive presents and toys, people in the town, rich and poor, old and young, were just like most of the people here today, sincere and kind, when they wished one another 'Happy Christmas', 'Peace on Earth and Goodwill to All'. And they all rose early on that Thursday, 25th December, and went to the Church of Ireland (now St. Paul's) where Rev. William Conyngham Plunket greeted them, or to the Catholic Church (now Holy Redeemer) where Rev. Alexander Roche led the happy congregation, rich and poor, in offering songs of joy and praise.

Let's go back further in time, to the year 1783, and have a look at what life was like then. That time too we were suffering one of our periodic famines and many were dying from hunger and disease. The American War of Independence was over, but we didn't yet know it because it took a long time for news to travel across the deep Atlantic Ocean. Grattan's Parliament was in existence and enjoying a certain amount of freedom from the British Parliament, although this didn't interest the thoughts or conversation of over ninety percent of the population as they weren't allowed to vote. The Ouzel Galley Society in Dublin had just recently changed it's name to the Dublin Chamber of Commerce. Christmas here was wretched and miserable. Nothing special, no luxuries, great poverty abounded, an unchanging diet of potatoes, sour milk, salt and perhaps dried fish. There was a scattering of small draughty cabins in Little Bray and on our Main Street and fishermen's cottages along the beach. The poor inhabitants had heard rumours of how their masters in Britain and in the big houses in Bray, and throughout Ireland, celebrate the joyful occasion - blazing fires to comfort those dwelling within, laughter, toys for children, the luxurious and expensive dinners, and the Christmas carols and services held in the churches saluting the infant Jesus. Here in Bray there was only the one church, now called St. Paul's (which is now today an organ factory). The peasants, living in the greatest poverty, would say their prayers and perhaps hope that a priest might come and celebrate Mass in one of their homes, there being no Catholic place of worship in the small town. Few could travel all the way to Kilmacanogue and back in their bare feet for Mass on Christmas Day, the nearest Catholic Chapel to Bray. But they were content, they had never been used to any other way of life. They were resigned to their lot, and were consoled with the thought that their reward for their suffering would come in the next life, which gave then the endurance to bear with this one. December 25th. 1783 was not to be like the other Christmases, it would be a celebration to remember for many years.

It was a dark night and, as usual at this time of year, there was a strong gale battering the coast, mountainous breakers rolled in from the sea and thundered along the deserted beach. There were no King's Revenue Men on the lookout that day, the weather being so bad that the contraband couldn't possibly be run ashore, so they were comfortably tucked up in their beds. A trading barque, that is a large ship with square sails on its fore and mainmast and the mizzen mast fore and aft rigged, named Friendship through some providential coincidence which traded regularly between the wealthy merchants of Bristol and Oporto, was bravely trying to ride out the gale on her voyage from Portugal to England with her holds filled with spices, fruits and rich wines. The tempest raged on and on, with the sound of the gale in the rigging screaming like a thousand devils, while the helmsman struggled to keep her head well out to sea; but the terrible storm overcame his valiant efforts and soon the vessel was off Bray's treacherous coast.

What the captain and crew feared most occurred: breakers on the port side, the shudder as the ship ran aground and the ensuing crashing of timbers and rigging. While fate had dealt them a cruel blow, their lives were not endangered; fortune had placed their vessel on the sand just out from where the Harbour Bar is now situated. There was no harbour there at that time, just a large estuary where the beautiful Dargle River meets the sea. The quickly-falling tide soon enabled the shipwrecked sailors to struggle ashore through the surf, and they soon lay exhausted on the dunes, where they gave thanks to God for their deliverance from drowning.

Mr. Quin's hotel had just been opened seven years before this, and it is likely that they were guided there and were given warmth, sympathy and hospitality, as is the custom the world over towards matelots who are cast upon the beaches.

Now, while this was going on, the sea had receded further; it was now possible to walk out to the abandoned ship, and there wasn't a sight or sound of any excise men or any other official with a crown in their uniform. Soon the word spread, and before long every pauper in Bray, that is most of the population, was unloading the cargo, men on board handing down the kegs and boxes to women and children who carried them off into the night. When the port and wines, the spices and the exotic fruits were rescued from the boat, the assembled multitude decided that the masts and ship's timbers should also be treated as a gift from providence, so they soon stripped the vessel until nothing remained.

Came the dawn and the ship's captain, the Revenue Men, the crew, and representatives of Bray's forces of law and order proceeded down to the sea to salvage the ship and its valuable cargo. They stood on the beach aghast. There wasn't a sign of a spar or a bit of flotsam, not even the smell of an open bottle of port. Oh what a wonderful Christmas that was in Bray!

Christmas and the great spectacle of the flashing colourful lights along our streets, placed there by the local Chamber of Commerce with the help of finance from the Bray traders, remind me of another story from the past.

THE CHAMBER OF COMMERCE

Our lovely town, though close to Dublin, still manages to retain its rural and individual characteristics; and one thing that brings this to mind is the wonderful decoration that we display at different times of the year. The whole shopping area is sometimes covered with gaily coloured pennants for the annual Bray Seaside and Family Festival, organised by a hard-working committee. Among the chairpersons of this committee were Father Tony Deane the founder, Alan Mulligan, Danny Bohan, John Nolan and Mary Doyle. Here in Bray, we also cover the streets at Christmas with a canopy of coloured lights; this splendid display of brilliant illumination is made possible through the good work of the local Chamber of Commerce. The Chamber of Commerce! Now there's a tale to tell. Let me aquaint you of its origins.

We go back to the year 1695 when a ship of ninety tons called the Ouzel, subsequently known as The Ouzel Galley, set sail from Ringsend under the command of Captain Eoghan Massey, bound for the Netherlands with a crew of forty experienced sailors. Their families all turned out on the quayside to bid them farewell and to wish them a speedy return. The wind was fair and all sails set as they passed within sight of Bray Head on their tranquil voyage down the Irish Sea, and they soon vanished over the horizon.

A year went by, their families awaited their expected return and began to worry. A further year passed, and by this time they were saying prayers for their missing loved ones. Another year elapsed, and their relatives and friends accepted the dreadful fact that all in the ship had perished; that their bones lay at the bottom of the ocean, or were bleaching on some scorched sand on a far away shore. The shipowners, Messrs Ferris Twiggs and Cash gave thanks to God that the venture had been insured and received full compensation for their loss.

Tempus fugit and behold, not a mirage but a miracle, there sailing past Bray Head and into Dublin came the Ouzel in the year 1700, five long years after it had set sail. Was it real? was it an apparition or a ghost ship? It was indeed, solid enough, with a wild looking, well-fed sunburnt and smiling crew and the holds filled with treasures, silks, spices and jewellery. The returned matelots were welcomed and cheered and all celebrated their safe return. Of course, everyone asked them what kept them away for so long. "Where were you and what in God's name did you do? The trouble we had when you were away, the prayers and Masses that we had said for your souls!" The heroes narrated a tale of wonder that amazed and enthralled their listeners. How they were captured and enslaved by fierce buccaneers and how, after many years, they managed to overpower their pirate masters and regain their vessel which, they joyfully found, was filled with booty and plunder. Everyone believed their tale, but in today's enlightened age the story sounds a bit far-fetched and there is a thought that perhaps it was the crew that turned to piracy. Another wonder is that no-one spilt the beans.

Who now owned the unexpected wealth? The crew? The shipowners? The insurers? A dispute arose immediately and arguments ensued for a number of years. Someone came up with a sensible idea. Pay the insurers back for the loss of the ship. As for the great treasure that it held, it would be pointless to continue arbitration, such procedure would only lead to the lawyers and barristers growing fatter at everyone's expense with their legal hocus pocus and long drawn our arguments. The crew decided that they would all join together and found a society which would help alleviate distress amongst Dublin merchants and arbitrate on disputes between them. And so, in the year 1705, the Ouzel Galley Society was formed.

The number of members was confined to forty, which was the original ship's complement, and they all had nautical titles: captain; gunner, gunner's mate, coxswain, lieutenant, bursar, carpenter, mate, boatswain, able seaman and so on. On the death of a member of the original crew, another merchant would be admitted to the ranks.

Now, don't for a moment think that their meetings were all serious and formal. They did resolve disputes; but most of the time their gatherings were held in convivial surroundings where they chatted, laughed, drank and generally had a good time. Maybe a bit like today. "Wife, I have a meeting to-night so I won't be home 'til late! God help you love, working so hard." The names of the places where they gathered aptly describe the seriousness of their meetings: Rose and Bottle Tavern in Dame Street, Phoenix Tavern in Werburgh Street, Ship Tavern in Chapelizod, Eagle Inn in Eustace Street and Atwell's Tavern in Dame Street.

The original wording of the formation of the society reads "For the Arbitration of all disputes to them referred relating to Trade and Commerce, the expenses whereof are apportioned to the benefit of decayed merchants". One of the rules was "The Captain or, in his absence, the Senior Officer on board, has supreme command at every meeting of the Galley, and any disobedience to him is mutiny".

The members supported Henry Grattan and gave their full approval to the motion "16th April 1782. Resolved that the King, Lords and Commons of

Ireland are solely competent to make laws for the government thereof and that we will pay obedience to such laws only as have received or shall receive their sanctions" . Dr. George Little, a former President of the Old Dublin Society, who was historian of the Ouzel Galley, described Ireland subsequent to the Act of Union.

> *Into our world stalked the Nineteenth Century. With it came the Act of Union, loss of trade, pestilence, famines and the reduction of a proud nation to the position of a poor relation. Of yore men had starved and died; now they still starved and died but not until they had been degraded first. Our city swarmed with the little men who grovelled for the little posts that sufficed their little pride. The colonial lords had fled the country with their wages of treachery and perjury tight-clutched.*

The Dublin Chamber of Commerce, founded in 1783, evolved from the Society, which continued to meet until the 1840s. It honours its history and origins by depicting the Ouzel Galley on its letter heading and the story is capsulated on its stationery. Towns, and cities throughout Ireland have followed these merchant's example, and here in Bray the Chamber of Commerce was established. Among the many members of the Ouzel Galley Society and the Dublin Chamber of Commerce who have had close associations with Bray were: David La Touche, Peter La Touche, William Digges La Touche, Joshua Pim, William Jameson and William Dargan. Not all of our societies or organisations have withstood the test of time.

One such comes to mind and is worthy of rememberance as it was very much part of Bray's history and contributed greatly to its social evolution. Let me tell you about it.

ST. KEVIN'S TONTINE BURIAL SOC.

"..and throwing down the pieces of silver in the temple, he departed; and he went and hanged himself. But the chief priests, taking the pieces of silver, said ' It is not lawful to put them into the treasury, since they are blood money '. So they took counsel, and bought with them the potter's field, to bury strangers in." (Matthew).

And the name 'Potters Field' is still used to-day all around the world to describe that part of the cemetery where those who are strangers and those who are destitute are buried.

Anytime you walk around Bray nowadays, you see the strange modern fashion, the self mutilation of young children, boys and men with ear rings. These rings hang in the oddest places, lips, navels and noses. (How do they blow their nose with a ring in it ?). It's not really a new thing because if you look at illustrations of 15th, 16th, 17th and sometimes 18th century sailors and pirates like Blackbeard, Kidd, Blood and Morgan, you will find that they are mostly depicted with a large gold ring, in their ear. This ring wasn't there for purely decorative purposes. You see, sailors were aware that the probability of being lost at sea was great, and that perhaps their bodies would be washed up on some foreign beach where they would be unknown. They dreaded the thought of being buried without ceremony in a 'Potter's Field' or worse still, being left for scavengers to dine on. So to allay their fears, they hoped and expected that the gold ear ring would pay for the cost of their interment. The dread or shame of being put into a pauper's grave, or not having sufficient money left to pay for the cost of a modest funeral, persisted to recent times, which is why, here in Bray, St. Kevin's Catholic Tontine Burial Society was founded in 1880 and survived until 1997. The name was changed in the early 1950s to St. Kevin's Burial Society. Collection of money from members was the main business of the Society, and this was originally conducted in an office at the Town Hall when it was newly built. Shortly after the small office was moved to the Trades Hall which is now the Bank of Ireland. Later, it was moved to the Connolly Hall, beside the Royal Hotel, and then to Church Terrace; from there it was moved back again to the Town Hall where they used the rent office. After that it was again moved, this time to the Court House, now the Heritage Centre, before moving once more to its final location in Holy Redeemer's Parish Centre. The organisation had no connection with the church, its members belonged to all parishes and religious denominations.

Terry Doyle was the last treasurer. He joined the Society in 1936, was Chairman from 1950 to 1989, and had two sons serving on the committee. His grandfather, William Kinsella, was one of the original founders, and ever since that, down through its existence of one hundred and seventeen years, there was always a member of his family on the committee.

The Society was registered under the Friendly Societies Act of 1896 and stated as its objects:

> *The Object of the Society is to ensure the payment of a sum of money on the death of a member or for the funeral expenses of the wife or husband of a member as the case may be. The Mortality payment is made in the case of a married member to the surviving partner and in the case of an unmarried member to the person nominated for such payment or to the next of kin. A husband and wife may hold separate membership cards but only one amount will be paid in the event of a death of either party. The Society will be open to all Irish Citizens.*

Church Terrace

Not alone did the Society provide the members with mortality benefit, but also it served as a means of saving. Each person usually withdrew their capital sum every December and the Society retained the interest earned which was accumulated and used for the members' funeral expenses and for the officers' wages. Because of the antiquity of its establishment in Bray, the names of those who were associated with it are a part of Old Bray's past. Their families have, for generations, contributed to its history. Serving on the last committee were Ned O'Brien (Asst. Sec.), Terry Doyle (Treasurer), Tom McManus (Sec.), Pat

Murphy (Chairman), Sean McGarry, Eamon Doyle, Sean Doyle, Marie O'Neill, Ray Flood and Alan McManus.

Unfortunately, some of the names of those who served the Society so well in the far distant past have faded into obscurity, but most are remembered. These were some of the officers: Chairmen: J. Shields (1900-1936), Pat Doyle (Terry's father, 1936-1950), Terry Doyle (1950-1989), Pat Murphy (1989-1995). Treasurers: Jack Murphy (1880-1935), Sam Hannon (1935-1989) and Terry Doyle; Secretaries: Harry Lyons (1903-1935), Joe Kenny (1936), Tom Mc Manus and Ned O'Brien.

The ordinary members down through the years were William Kinsella, J. Shields and Jack Murphy (all from 1880); Harry Lyons, Pat Doyle, Jack Hannon, Tom Byrne and Jack Murphy (all from 1900-1935); Sam Hannon, Pat Doyle, Jack Murphy, Joe Kenny, George Byrne, Jack Hannon, Christy Brien, Pat Murphy, Eddie Furlong, Fred Curtis, Peter Doyle, Harry Lyons, Frank Darcy and Brendan Richardson (all from 1935-1950.)

In 1980 a terrible thing occurred! Some horrible miscreants or gurriers robbed the Society as it was receiving the cash from the members. These lowest of the lowest class of thieves were armed with a shotgun, which they discharged in the course of their heinous crime, but luckily no one was injured. The miserable dregs of humanity escaped with the loot, which, I imagine didn't bring them much luck. How could it? After all they had, in a sort of way, robbed the dying.

The Society ceased to exist because the Bray Credit Union served the members more attractively, and also because of the reduction of interest rates for deposits in all banking institutions.

1846

The Bray Heritage Centre is situated in the old courthouse (1841) outside the Royal Hotel. Within, there are exhibits giving details of Bray's past which tourists find entertaining and interesting. There are also other objects which are just dust collectors and that have nothing to do with Bray. The greatest thing about this centre is it's hard-working committee, under the chairmanship of Councillor Noel Keyes, who arrange different exhibitions throughout the year and also organise lectures, many of which are worthwhile attending. A nominal cover charge for admission to the lectures is sometimes asked, but this is compensated for by free wine and cheese.

In 1996 there was an exhibition in the Centre to commemorate the appalling hunger that occurred from 1846 onwards, and it presented the full horror of that terrible time. One of the events that happened in January of 1846, on the first Saturday of that new year to be exact, was the visit of the Lord Mayor and aldermen of Dublin to Windsor in order to deliver a petition to Queen Victoria. Immediately prior to their audience with her, she had received a deputation from the Lord Mayor and representatives of London. It turned out that this episode in history was regarded with some humour by the popular English press for the following reason.

The London delegation, even though they were aware that an extravagant and mouth-watering repast awaited them in the royal palace, had broken their journey and had dined on the way, thinking that they'd have sufficient time to do justice to both meals. The food prepared by the royal cook for the mayor and his companions was described as "a most sumptuous collation served on a long range of tables, extending round the sides, and covered with the greatest variety of refreshments and delicacies. The centre of each table was elegantly ornamented with handsome silver vases richly chased and with a number of ornamental designs. The Queen's pages attended at the tables on the guests supplying the numerous party with champagne and other choice wines".

The guests from London, who were now late for their audience because they had stopped on their way in order to stuff their faces with food, were confronted with this appetising, mouth-watering display before being admitted to their monarch's presence. They now had only time to nibble at the starters before they were called and ushered into Victoria's presence where they delivered their eloquent words, which were received with the usual comforting platitudes before they said good bye and were sent on their way back to London.

Along came the Dublin party at 2.30 p.m., in plenty of time because they hadn't stopped and were now very, very hungry. Before seeing the queen they demolished all the food that was displayed.

This singular event was marked by the composition of a poem which amused the readers of the popular press, though there wasn't much laughter in Ireland!:

There's agitation at Paddington Station,
For the London and Dublin Corporation
With their brace of Lord Mayors,
And town council in pairs,
Are bound to Windsor on weighty affairs.
They bear a petition
For Royal permission
And London's deputies nothing loath,
Count at dining at Slough and Windsor both.
But Dublin is wiser, and rather than stop,
They take the omnibus, jump on the top,
With swords, robes and maces,
In big packing cases.
Oh didn't the Alderman's mouth overflow?
And didn't they curse their first luncheon at Slough?
And didn't they fume as the chaplain said grace,
And mentally pray that he'd quicken his pace?
When just as they're starting,
Sir William Martin
Pops his head in to say,
"My Lord Mayor, step in this way-
Her Majesty waits, and you've no time to stay".
No hopes their appetites of sating,
They follow the gentlemen ushers in waiting.
Meanwhile the Corporation of Dublin
Had wisely saved themselves the trouble in
Solving such question, by tucking in double, in
Waterloo Hall,
Where waiters and all,
Their Milesian appetites hugely appal;
They prove to the Saxon,
If he lays a tax on
Irishmen's bellies, and on Irishmen's backs on

Such a chance of vengeance is not to be lost,
At a luncheon at Windsor, at Royal cost.
Not the great Liberator
Could wish for a greater
Triumph of Erin o'er Saxon Arch-traitor;
For the Lord Mayor and corporate body of London
By their Dublin brethern are fairly undone;
Had they even come back through Waterloo Hall,
They'd have found the fragments, and that had been all;
For never did Aldermen manage quicker
to empty the dishes and floor the liquor."

So you see everyone had a good laugh except the Irish, and it was little wonder; the words delivered to the queen were deadly serious:

The danger that exists of a whole people under your Majesty's sway falling victims to the scourge of famine and pestilence if measures shall not be promptly taken by your Majesty's Government, under the blessing of a merciful God, to avert from Ireland such a calamity. They have been reduced for many, very many years to look to the potato crop as the only source from whence to draw their daily sustenance. To them, beyond the people of all other nations, was assigned, as their only food, the poorest food in the world, and of that, for the vast majority of them, their supply was scanty; but their wretchedness did not terminate even at this point; for them there was still a step lower in their depths of misery. Their supply of food was not only scanty and of the worst kind, but of late years they were compelled to eke out an existence on the very worst species of their food- alas! food unfitted for the brute animal was and is the food of the vast majority of your subjects in Ireland. More than four millions of human beings, whose only food is the potato, whose only drink is water, whose houses are pervious to the rain, to whom a bed or a blanket is a luxury unknown and who are more wretched than any other people in Europe. Who are on the verge of famine, and this related of the inhabitants of a country which, of late years, may be justly termed the granary of England, exporting annually from the midst of a starving population food of the best kind in sufficient abundance for treble its own inhabitants.

There was an abundance of material prepared and displayed at that exhibition, the tragic contemporary poetry, eviction scenes, soup kitchens, coffin ships and everything that helped recall the tragedy.

BRAY IN THE EARLY 1900S

Let the time roll back to the early part of the twentieth century, while we take a leisurely stroll through the streets of Bray and view the retail establishments of the past - before plastic, chrome and neon signs were invented - to the days when the shop fronts were decorated with carved wood and there were bevelled plate glass mirrors with the names of the traders engraved in gold: to the infancy of that century when there was no traffic congestion and the world and its inhabitants moved without haste. Let's travel back and journey on a tour where we will be the ghosts from the present visiting the reality of a bygone age.

We commence on the Main Street where there remain some small thatched cottages near the recently-built Town Hall. The gutters at both sides of the

Main Street

street are filled with round cobble stones, well polished by millions of footsteps and the wheels of horse-drawn carriages. Small gas lampposts are situated occasionally in pavements all edged with granite, one six-sided letterbox with the initials of the monarch who ruled at the time of its construction is the only apparent piece of street furniture. There are occasional troughs, enabling horses to quench their thirst, and pumps and fountains of fresh clean water for the inhabitants. A small sign of mistrust is apparent as the drinking cup, made of cast iron, is attached to the fountains by means of a steel chain. The road is comprised of earth and gravel.

Where does the noise come from? The clang and bang and the sound of metal on metal, reminding us of the 'Anvil Chorus' from Il Trovatore. We are beside the forge of Mr. Furlong, who is working away hammering the iron on his anvil with steady rhythmic strokes beside his furnace. Around him lie examples of his art such as wrought-iron gates embellished with intricate floral patterns, horse shoes, hoops for carriage wheels, railings and garden seats for the fine houses of the gentry. (The fire has now gone out and the blacksmiths art is no longer practised here since Jack Furlong passed away in the 1990s).

On the opposite side of the street, at number 50, there is the grocer and spirit merchant Patrick Shannon famed for his best drinks and hospitality to strangers. The two windows on front of the shop display his tempting wares, one being filled with culinary items for the table, the other with a shining array of twinkling coloured bottles. (This establishment is now occupied by Mr. Ken Duff, who dispenses hospitality behind his bar and lounge. Two windows remain to-day and they display momentos and memorabilia of that vanished age).

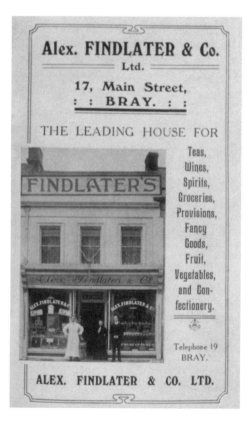

Back at the far side of the road again we find Jack Ryan, another grocer and spirit merchant, whose knowledge of fine wines and beers is legendary. Mr. Ryan and his curate still wear the Victorian striped blue apron which is the traditional uniform of his trade. (He too has now long faded into history but the thriving business continues under the capable supervision of Mr. Syl. Holland, ex Hon. Lord Mayor of Bray, who is now the genial host and proprietor.)

The modern structure at number four, with its two large windows and carved wooden surround in true Victorian fashion, is occupied by Frederick Jacob, who is an ironmonger and a cycle agent. The goods on display in one window offer all that might be required in any large kitchen, and the other offers two bicycles, one for a lady complete with wicker basket and covering over the rear wheel to prevent the long skirt getting caught in the spokes. Establishments selling bicycles have become more numerous since this popular mode of rapid transport became fashionable. (Mr Jacob has long gone but Mr. Andrew Ledwidge, who comes from an old and honourable Bray family, is now the owner of the building where he stocks an infinite variety of hardware and household goods at very reasonable prices and the personal attention he gives his customers is reminiscent of those far off days. He has preserved the appearance of his building and it remains a wonderful example of early 20th century architecture and design.)

Directly opposite, beside the church, at number 97 is the shop of Malachi Mackey, spirit merchant and pork butcher. Being situated nearest to Church of Most Holy Redeemer, it is a refuge and haven for grieving mourners where they find solace and sympathy before and after funerals. (This became the Widow Ward's before becoming known as the Glenmalure which was in turn owned by Dick McGahan and Gerry Ryan. It is no longer a public house.)

Not far away, at number 90, is the shop of Mrs. Catherine Smyth, later to become Dempsey Brothers, which sells fresh meat and game. The permanent fixed canopy, with its iron slats from which the sides of prime beef and lamb hang, covers the pavement and is most welcome to idle gossipers on an inclement day. (This victualler's establishment is now owned by Frank Doyle who is proud of the fact that he has preserved the appearance.)

Across the road again and we come to another grocer and spirit merchant, Mr. Dick Bolger. His shop's design is similar to other establishments with the grocery section in the front and the imbibing area at the rear. The air is heavy with smoke from the patrons' pipes, and the aroma from these, together with the heavy odour of ale and stout is no different from that which prevails in other bars. All these floors are made up of bare wooden boards which are sprinkled with sawdust and swept out daily. (This is no longer a licensed premises but is now Dickers Electrical, where Mary offers a modern range of audio and visual equipment, as well as a wide selection of communication devices.)

And here at number 82 and 83 is displayed inside the work of the woodcarvers, the name over the portal reads 'Bray Art Furniture' . Our town is famous for this work, and fine examples of their art can be seen in the churches surrounding us for all worshippers to admire. Christ Church on Church Road, opposite The Rectory (where now Rev. Baden Stanley resides), possesses the best; the little Church of Ireland at the end of the Herbert Road is also decorated with many fine pieces. Holy Redeemer's sacristy has two oak chairs, unique in design, made by them. (The Bray Woodcarvers premises still survive, but today they are now occupied by the E.S.B.) Mr. George Pierce, grocer and vintner, is at number 45, beside the entrance to St. Cronan's, which is occupied by Dr. Donnelly Parish Priest of Bray and Bishop of Canea.

We are near number 1, the large establishment of Messers Leverett and Fry, grocers and wine merchants. Oh what a pleasant aroma greets us and soothes our sense of smell, as we enter the doorway on to the tiled floor which is freshly sprinkled with sawdust. The scent of the large open chests of tea, the smoked hams hanging from the wooden ceiling, the slabs of butter on the white marble counters, dried fruit, raisins and spices from the far orient. Displayed all around are the most succulent and tempting variety of grocery items.

Being in the vicinity of the Quinsboro Road, our eyes behold the shopfront of

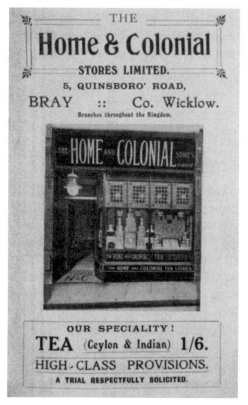

Mr. Gethings who occupies number 14. We pass through the entrance, first removing the mud off our boots with the help of the shoescraper which is in the pavement outside the shop, and what do we find? A veritable Alladin's cave of treasures too numerous to list. The windows and display cabinets are filled with the twinkling of cut glass and the shining of fine Beleek porcelain. (Now, alas, no longer there, it too has faded like all else into the dim memories of the distant past.)

Doran's Medical Hall, established in 1849 at number 1 Goldsmith Terrace isn't far away. Within, on numerous shelves, are hundreds of glass bottles filled with powders which will eventually be mixed by the chemist with the help of the pestle and mortar that sits on the counter. This shop is in competition with Raverty's Medical Hall at 110 Main Street. All patent medicines of repute, as well as accurately compounded prescriptions, can be purchased in both premises.

Our feet are tired and it's time we rested our weary bones and now that we're in the proximity of Mrs. Christina Heffernon's tea-rooms and restaurant at number 35, we will take this opportunity to sit down and enjoy what she has to offer. The tables are covered with fine linen tablecloths bordered with Carrickmacross lace. The teapot matches the cups and is made of the finest bone china. The young lady serving is dressed in a long black costume, with a white starched apron and a small lace hat to match. No tea bags here but highest quality leaves from India and Ceylon, and the fresh cream comes from the dairy of John Neil, whose retail premises occupy numbers 61 and 62.

Now that we're refreshed, and our limbs capable of withstanding further exercise, let us proceed to the furthest extremities of the north-east part of our town - the harbour, which isn't long opened to shipping, the first beacon shining in the lighthouse, at the end of the south pier, in 1897. There are no shops in the neat row of fishermen's cottages at Dock Terrace. Mr. Dick Kenna occupies numbers 1, 2 and 3, where he sells wines, spirits and ales in the premises known as the Harbour Saloon, a long-established inn dating back to the early days of the previous century and, a safe haven for seafarers. We enter into the dim light and find the landlord, who welcomes us and serves us with samples of the house special, Guinness porter and Guinness stout. Time passes too quickly and we must depart. (Des and Paul O'Toole now own this famous house.)

Our tour of Great Bray is now at an end, there are many more establishments worthwhile visiting, but time prohibits their inclusion for the moment. Instead we will continue our walk and have a look at Little Bray.

This part of the town was sometimes called Bray Minor and in some church documents 'Bray Inferior'. Well, there's nothing minor or inferior about the place, and most people from Big Bray come here to stay – this is where the cemetery is. We'll commence our random tour in Castle Street, so named because of the Castle which is opposite to Mr. Robert Foley's saddle and harness maker's establishment, which has a stuffed pony in the window. The castle served as a barracks for the police around 1837 and now it's a private residence. The street was officially named in 1808 and the name is carved on that stone which you can see, up there, on Pat Byrne's licensed premises beside the laneway. (We will conclude our visit here later after partaking in some of the nourishment that he has to offer.) Here also is the forge of William Smith, the shop of Mrs. Clifton, who also sells wines and spirits, and the stable and workshop of Frank Denehey the coachbuilder. Heitons have the large building and yard from which they sell coal and timber, which they imported to Bray in their own steamships. Up the street a bit on this side of the river, is the Church of Ireland national school. We'll stroll across the road and beware of the horse traffic. There's the fast and speedy coach and four which still travels from Dublin and goes as far as Greystones. This coach is called the 'Shamrock' and will soon be made obsolete by the new rapid form of transport - the motor carriage.

The park, with the beautiful lodge which is similar in style to our Town Hall up in Big Bray, was presented to the citizens by the Earl of Meath a few years ago, and provides recreation for the youth of the area. The large building facing the park, on the Dargle Road, is the Cripples Home founded in 1874. Within there's a memorial plaque which reads "Home for destitute crippled children founded by Lucinda Sullivan 1874 as a thanks offering to Almighty God for deliverance from peril of shipwreck on the Lake of Zurich August 19th. 1872". Mrs. Morris is presently in charge of the young people, many of whom are in invalid carriages. On this road is the home of the builder Tom Dodd and that shop, with the bread and cakes in the window, is the bakery of Short Brothers (is everything sold here called 'shortbread'?). And here in 'Sugarloaf View' is Henry Byrne who supplies many houses with fresh fruit and vegetables. 'Mill View' is so named because it faces the brewery of Watkins' Jameson and Pim. Just across the river is Mr. Ben Heazle, who is a rate and rent collector, not the most popular occupation but he acquits himself well by his gentle manner. The area around here is filled with little streets and small neat comfortable dwellings. Maitland Street has three railway men,

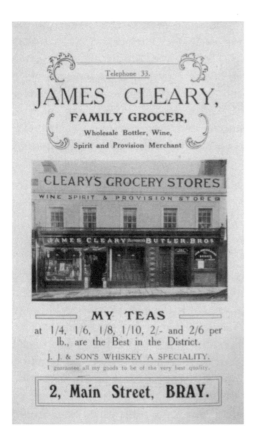

Mr.Goggin in number 30, Mr.Mooney in number 27 and Mr. Fortune at number 36. (Fortune is an old Bray name and many reside here to-day. Shay Fortune is the proprietor of an excellent printing and design establishment, down over the level crossing and behind the railway station.) Dargan Street is the abode of Richard Hudson, who is a master carpenter in number 1, and a famous coachman, James Byrne, resides at number 9. In number 29 is a Mr. T. Brabazon who, when he is imbibing spirituous liquor, jokingly informs his listeners that, because of his name, he should be living in Kilruddery. In Ardee Street, named after the Earl of Meath's son, you'll find Mr. Pratt at No. 8, who is a groom, an occupation that is fast vanishing. John Caffrey lives in number 5 and Mr. Gavin, a market gardener, dwells in number 18. Greenpark Road has two residents much admired by all children, James Leggett, an engine driver and nearby is Francis McClean, a master mariner who has been around The Horn. Dargle View Terrace gives shelter to Patrick Keenan, a carpenter, at number 2. Thomas Dempsey, a coachbuilder, is in number 4 and Patrick Egan, who has decorated and painted the inside of St. Peter's also lives there. Let us now venture further afield, but before doing so we can refresh ourselves in Mrs. Annie Brooks tea rooms at number 2 Dargle Road.

On the Upper Dargle Road, there is John Sutton (another very old Bray name), the builder, and William Embledge who is in competition with him, although they are good friends. In Sutton Villas at number 5 is John O'Rourke, who is a member of the R.I.C. Here on the Dublin and Kingstown Road is the licensed premises of Pat Corry and the convalescent home, with Miss Lyons as matron, established in 1881 as part of the Meath Hospital, also called after the Brabazons, in Dublin. The Elliot Home for orphans isn't far, away and there's plenty of milk for the children provided from the dairy of Andrew Brien which is nearby. The driveway at the far side of the road leads to the residence of Sir Edward Wingfield, who lives in Corke Abbey.

At Old Connaught is Lord Plunket (spelt with one 't') in Old Connaught House, Dr. Wilkinson in Jubilee Hall, Miss Revington in Palermo and Dr. Hear is in Thornhill. At Crinken resides Miss Bookey in Beauchamp and Sir Stanley Herbert Cochrane lives nearby (of mineral water fame through the firm of Cantrell and Cochrane, now known as simply 'C&C'). Cochrane has opened a new cricket ground at Woodbrook, and a pleasant Sunday afternoon may be spent here viewing the sport from a deckchair on the veranda of the pavilion. Jolly good show and all that! While on the subject of sport, I must mention that visitors are welcome at the golf links when introduced by a member and the green fee is a modest one shilling and six pence. Mr Richard Larkin is the professional who coaches members. There is some talk of ladies playing the game, but I do think that, like the franchise, such an idea is preposterous. It's time we went back towards the town. Over there are the gates of Ravenswell Convent, which is the home of the Sisters of Charity who acquired it a few years ago. Before that they were in St. Peter's Presbytery, locally known as 'Rack Rent House'. The good nuns taught religious instruction in St. Peter's National School and now, in their new and more spacious premises, having converted some large stables, they have a new school which can accommodate 300 pupils. Ravenswell and the vicinity used to be called Bloodybank because of a great battle fought there in 1402, when the O'Byrnes were defeated. The name, not being conducive towards tourism, has now been changed to 'Sunnybank'. There are many more interesting details about Little Bray, but time flies and so we must away and hope to return soon.

Fatigue makes it difficult to reach the outskirts of the town where we dwell, so having dispatched a boy from the saloon of Pat Byrne's alehouse in Castle Street, to the stable of Martin Doyle in Albert Avenue, where he has many fine carriages for hire, we will soon be collected and brought to our respective homes. We bid you adieu, and leave the past, to wake up in the noisy, tumultuous and speeding present.

The reader has, without doubt, wondered about the large numbers of 'watering holes' that were here then, even today there are a total of thirty two where alcoholic drink may be partaken on the premises. This reminds me of what it was like two centuries ago. Let me tell you about it.

ALEHOUSES 200 YEARS AGO

About two centuries ago, the parishioners of the Established Church in Bray and throughout the country were empowered by an Act of Parliament to appoint persons whose function was to inspect premises selling beers, wines and spirits, and to remove any person found drinking in them at 'unseasonable' hours. The authority of these overseers was the same as that of constables and peace officers and they were to ensure, among other things, that no alcohol was sold on Sundays before four o'clock in the afternoon. These 'Inspectors' patrolled Bray and it's environs, and levied the penalties imposed by law on the transgressors. The amount collected from these fines was distributed to their own favourite charities. One of their other functions was to enquire in detail into the character of persons who were permitted to keep public houses or inns, and the findings of their investigations were given to the local magistrates. Reference was made to the various houses as 'dram shops' or 'tippling premises', and the inspectors publicised details of the ' immorality and misery that prevailed among the lower orders in consequence of the excessive use of spirituous liquors'. They attempted to have these closed all day on Sunday, it being the Sabbath, and they condemned the revolutionary government of France who had abolished Sunday from their calendar, which action they referred to as one of 'daring impiety'.

The town of Bray was growing fast and there were many respectable pubs, as well as the usual traditional disreputable sheebeens. A map made by John Taylor in 1816 indicates that the town was catering for a large community, and that even twenty years before, visits of those who lived in the surrounding countryside were increasing: therefore some control of the laws relating to drink was required. One of the tracts issued at the time reads:

> *One of the greatest evils under which this country labours is the relaxation or non execution of existing laws. It would be unfair to impute this laxity of public discipline to the magistrates alone. It cannot be doubted that this widely extended evil with all it's pernicious consequences to the peace, order and happiness of society, to the civilisation of the lower, and the security of the higher orders would vanish in a few years if the efforts of the inhabitants to support the laws made for their own protection should begin to outrun the zeal of the magistracy it might then be pronounced with confidence that the day of civilisation had arrived and that the remnants of barbarism which had hitherto overspread the face of the country, would speedily vanish before it.*

Later on, subsequent to the rising of 1798, it was noted that "during the rebellion the magistrates experienced the good effects resulting from a variety of instances, their accurate state and character of the several public houses, were of the utmost importance in enabling them to counteract the machinations of treason and sedition".

Despite these proud words the good intentions of these overseers or inspectors (or spies) didn't meet with any great success and they soon faded into oblivion.

And what were the comforts provided by these dens of iniquity? In order to sample the atmosphere that prevailed within, a visit to Clancy's, on the Quinsboro Road, or the Harbour Bar perhaps, will give you an idea about the decor in those days. Places where men could mix and converse with their peers in convivial surroundings. The comfort of an open fire on a cold winter's night with the reflection of the flames dancing on the walls. The shadows from the light of the candles and oil lanterns. The exchange of stories, gossip and news. Fears, hopes and problems were discussed, advice freely given by 'mine host' and gratefully received by the customer. Pewter tankards, on wooden tables, filled with first and second run ale from the local brewery, or glasses of ruby and gold coloured wine and uisce beatha for those that preferred strong spirits. The landlord or his 'curate' would busy themselves, when custom was slack, by tapping the wooden firkins or hogsheads and bottling the contents.

Military bands and small orchestras, which provided entertainment in the grand hotels, were absent from these small establishments and instead the customers, with their fiddles and uilleann pipes, combined their talents to render the happy strains of their native jigs and reels, while sometimes a sad lament would be played. These Irish airs can still be heard in Bray when refuge from the world's cares is sought within such pleasant hostelries as Cois Farraige, Clancy's and The Mayfair.

TRAVELLING AND TRANSPORT

Up to around 1815, the hazards of travelling long distances were great and it was confined chiefly to mail coaches and a few day coaches that ran on main roads. It was only the very wealthy that could afford the luxury of such travel as the cost was great, so the poor and the ordinary people had to walk. If a long journey was undertaken by coach, it was not unusual for the brave adventurer to settle his affairs and make a will before setting out on the perilous expedition. This was to change with the arrival of Mr. Charles Bianconi, who established a business in Clonmel in 1815 and introduced his 'public cars', which were soon to become familiar to the people of Bray, as they passed through the town daily.

He started his service with one wagon in 1815 and by 1843 he had 110 vehicles on the roads each one capable of carrying up to 20 passengers. They travelled at a speed of 8 to 9 miles an hour and the average fare charged was a penny farthing a mile. Bray to Dublin return was about three shillings (15 new pence), which was the average weekly wage for many a good labourer (just imagine the furore today if the Dart or Dublin Bus were to ask you for £200!). His wagons covered 3,800 miles in total daily, and they passed through 140 stops where his horses were refreshed and changed. The animals numbered 1,200 and consumed 3,500 tons of hay and 35,000 barrels of oats annually. Of course, having 110 wagons meant that he had more than that number of drivers, not to mention the grooms, blacksmiths, carpenters, wheelwrights and clerks. He was one of the largest employers in the country.

Bianconi was a severe but just person, and any one of his workers who was found guilty of a misdemeanour or falsehood was instantly dismissed. On the other hand, he looked after those who served him faithfully by paying them their full wage for life after their retirement or illness. He also helped maintain their dependants.

Roads in Bray in those days were untarred; made of earth and rough stones they changed to mud in the rain. Constant horse traffic made it worse as manure mixed with the mud, so that pedestrians were splashed by the wheels of the vehicles going up and down our Main Street. Ends and hems of the early Victorian dresses very rapidly became soiled and dirty, and to try and combat this problem large granite slabs, were inserted in the roads, at crossing points between footpaths, for people to walk on. It was usual for a man or boy to attend nearby and to sweep these slabs thus clearing the way in front of any lady who looked as if she might reward the service with a farthing, or the great charity of a halfpenny. An example of these stones still remain at the top of the Florence Road opposite to Holy Redeemer.

Charles Bianconi provided his service six days a week and no vehicles travelled on Sundays. He gave two reasons for this in his own words, "that the Irish, being a religious people, will not travel on business on Sundays. My experience taught me that I can work a horse eight miles a day for six days better than six miles for seven days".

Soon all was to change again with the spread of the railway throughout Ireland, and with the great starvation and pestilence which was soon to decimate the countryside. Bianconi faded into history in his own lifetime.

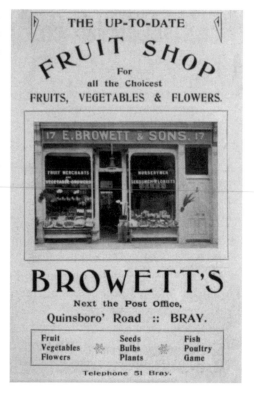

THE UP-TO-DATE

FRUIT SHOP

For all the Choicest

FRUITS, VEGETABLES & FLOWERS.

17 E. BROWETT & SONS. 17

BROWETT'S

Next the Post Office,
Quinsboro' Road :: BRAY.

Fruit	Seeds	Fish
Vegetables	Bulbs	Poultry
Flowers	Plants	Game

Telephone 51 Bray.

What a change there is in Bray's traffic today, with over-congestion, emission of petrol and diesel fumes from clapped-out lorries, buses and bangers. Traffic lights, the fear beating in the pedestrian's breast as they try and cross the road, the awful fright that we get as we are narrowly missed by some driver who tries to beat the red, the dreadful noise from all the engines, which may be making us more deaf than any Irish soldier who sued the State. Less than a century ago it was very different. There was the sound of music on the streets of Bray, no one was in a hurry, the noise was a symphony of the melodious jingle of harnesses, the whinnying of a protesting animal, gentle shouts of encouragement from drivers to horses that only the creature could understand - G'up! Whoa! and the peculiar noise of the tongue clicking against the roof of the driver's mouth, the whistle, the rattle of the iron rimmed wheels on the cobblestones, the rhythm of hoofs going 'clip-clop' when the speed was slow and 'clippity-clippity-clop' when the horse was urged to hurry, which wasn't very often. Conveniently placed all around the town were numerous troughs filled with clear fresh water, from which the animals quenched their thirst while

Jarvies and Enniskerry Coach

their drivers engaged one another in idle conversation. Up some of the laneways and side streets, you can still find the stables, some now converted to mews residences, where the noble beasts retired in the evenings for their well-earned rest. The life and business of Bray depended on the well-being of these horses and so they were properly cared for.

Down at the station, the area where you now see buses and parked cars, was known as 'the yard' and in those days, it was enclosed by large gates, within which there were numerous carriages awaiting passengers from the trains. Tourists were well catered for, as excursions from the station were available in traps drawn by one and sometimes two horses at reasonable fares. For example you could take an excursion to Glendalough and back for 16 shillings (80 new pence), which covered 4 passengers in great comfort. A jarvey would charge 5 shillings (25 new pence) to go to Delgany, or if your destination was Old Connaught, beside Bray, the price was a mere shilling (5 new pence).

And did you wonder sometimes about the two feet high round granite pillars, tapering at the top, which are at the corners of some laneways and entrances to the large houses ? There are some people that will inform you that these were for people of small stature to stand on so that they might mount their steeds. Absolute rubbish, the real reason was to stop the carriage wheels being jammed, preventing the hub or axle striking the wall as it turned a corner. Mind you, there is no doubt that little people did use them to get up on their horses, but that wasn't their original function. These horses and carriages were big business in our town and gave employment to many. I set out the occupations, names and addresses of some of those who were engaged in this work and wonder do their descendants still dwell at the same address. Some of the houses, like the people, have vanished into the distant past.

Livery Stables :	M. Traynor & Sons,	Albert Avenue
	Martin Doyle, do	
Carriers and Carters :	John Ryan,	Westview Terrace,
	Pat Fitzsimons,	52A Main Street
	Andrew Byrne,	Greenpark Road
Groom :	Mr. Pratt	of Ardee Street
Saddlers :	George Blackburn,	68 Main Street
	Robert Foley,	Castle Street
Coach & Carriage Builders :	William Porter,	112 Main Street
	John Thompson,	Fairgreen
	Dave Towson,	16 Castle Street
	Frank Denehy,	Castle Street
	Tom Dempsey,	4 Dargle View Terrace
Shoeing and General Smith :	Joe Smith,	Castle Street
	Sam Smith,	do
Farriers :	Joe Furlong,	53 Main Street
	Mrs. M. Devitt,	89 Main Street
	John Doyle,	Crinken
Coachmen :	Willie Doyle,	63 Main Street
	Denis Doyle,	Newtown, Vevay
	Dan Nolan,	Lauderdale Terrace
	Mick O'Toole,	Myrtle Cottage, Vevay Rd
	Christy Grey,	3 Dargle Terrace
	T. Patterson,	2 Brabazon Ctgs, Dargle Rd.
	Mick Quin,	5 Dargan Terrace
	Jimmy Byrne,	9 Dargan Street

We look back with nostalgia at those far off days.... Mr. Foley's shop in Castle Street with the stuffed horse in the window and inside the wonderful aroma of leather and wax......the polished brasses on the harness and the occasional bell gently jingling as the horse moved.... and the way they looked at you with their large intelligent eyes.... and we talked to them and I believe that they understood what we said. Now all are gone and we're left with our motor cars, which reminds me of the time when Bray made an attempt to manufacture a mechanical propelled vehicle.

It's difficult to conjure up in your mind what the place was like at the turn of nineteenth century, no traffic jams, plenty of parking space, no traffic regulations, plenty of room for everyone to wander willy nilly about. The motor car was just about to make its appearance. These horseless carriages must have been a most extraordinary sight when they first spluttered up past St. Paul's and along Main Street on their way to the homes of the rich and famous. (Mr. Syl Holland of Holland's Lounge has a few examples of these, and perhaps if you drop in to partake of some refreshment he might bring you for a run in one of them). Which reminds me, I must tell you about one of the first of these in Bray.

The Agricultural and Technical Instruction (Ireland) Act was passed in 1899 and subsequently on Thursday December 20 at 10.30 am a meeting was held in the Town Hall to establish the aims of this act. Those present and representing the council were: Sir Henry Cochrane, J. Plunkett, J. E. McCormick, P. Robinson, N. Langton, J. W. Reigh, P. Condrin and W. Bryan. Also present and appointed to the committee were: Dr. Nicholas Donnelly, Bishop of Canea, Venerable Archdeacon Scott, Rev. H. P. Glenn, Rev. Father Colahan, J. Coughlan, The Earl Of Meath described in the minutes as ' Lord of the Manor', Rt. Hon. Viscount Powerscourt, Rt. Hon. Viscount Monck, A.McDonnell (plumber), P. J. Rossiter (printer), W. Smith (smith worker), N. Ryan (builder) and J. Sutton (builder).

Soon afterwards, when the old Queen and Empress of India had just passed away, that mechanical miracle that was to change the world had just made its appearance on the streets and most of the inhabitants were saying "They'll never catch on! They're just a passing fancy! Can't last! Not dependable! The pony and trap is safer and will always be there when needed!" But there were some persons who felt that the new horseless carriages might have advantages and that they deserved a closer look.

By this time, the Bray Technical Instruction Committee had changed its name to the Bray Agriculture and Technical Instruction Committee, and was well established and responsible for teaching technology and all sorts of modern trades. At a meeting in their school at Brighton Terrace (close to where A.J.Edge Ltd now have their premises) on 26 June 1903, there were present: Rev. Nicholas Donnelly, Archdeacon Scott, Father Colahan, J.W. Reigh and V.C. Le Fanu of the U.D.C. Gathered around the table they deliberated on such courses as knitting, crochet and lace classes, woodcarving and cottage industries. A petition from the residents of Brighton Terrace (where Pat O'Toole now resides), requesting that the mature trees be felled, as they regarded them as an eyesore, was read. It was warm and close; the voices droned on and on in monotonous tones, a few present half-listened and half dozed. Suddenly their interest was aroused. MOTOR CAR? Did he say MOTOR CAR? The secretary was certainly talking about such a new and rapid form of transport, and what he proposed was to occupy the committee's time for many months and eventually for years. "LET'S BUILD A MOTOR CAR!" He suggested that a workshop class be equipped for this purpose, and that twenty four tradesmen be found who would be willing to devote their spare time to enable this ambition become a reality. Before long the following names with their respective trades were enrolled (perhaps your grandfather's is here):

Fitters: John O'Brien, Thomas O'Brien, James Lynch, Chris Coates.
Engineering Apprentices : J. O'Brien, T. Tomlinson. Blacksmiths: J. Devitt, R. Collins, L. Rooney. Smith's Helper: J. Pepper. Coachbuilder: J. Gorman. Vicemen: I. Hunt. C. Farrell. Wheeler: J. Doyle. Coach body maker: W. Barrington. Apprentice coach body maker: W. Thompson & J. Waldon. Coach painter: James & John Carroll. Carpenters: John Thompson. Carriage and wheel worker: P. Berry. Tinsmith: F. O'Reilly. Ironmonger and cycle repairer: J. Wolfe.

The secretary proposed that the car should not be sold but "should be kept and used as a means of providing instruction in the care and management of a car to many whose chances of employment, in the service of motor car owners, would be improved by such knowledge."

Now, with such an array of talent, I cannot but wonder at the nature of the vehicle they intended to construct. It would, perhaps, look more like a horse drawn carriage with a combustion engine attached. Wooden wheels with solid rubber around the rims, leather upholstery and exotic hard wood panelling, brilliant colours in the enamel work completed by the carriage painter. How many would it accommodate when it made its first journey up Bray's Main Street? Perhaps the entire class. Would they give it a name ? Dr. Donnelly's Comet? Their dream went on and on, until.

The technical school was dependent on the Department of Agriculture and Technical Instruction for Ireland to provide them with the finance to enable them to purchase tools for the Mechanical Engineering class so that their worthy scheme could proceed. Alas, no grant was forthcoming and the plans had to be modified and become less ambitious.

At a meeting on 12th November 1903, it was resolved that the plan should be changed and a more moderate one implemented. "That a Daimler car of modern type be secured on hire, that a sufficient supply of hand tools be procured, that a competent motor engineer be engaged and that a class be formed for the training of motor drivers". Father Colahan made approaches to Huttons, leaders in the field of motor cars at that time, and it was arranged that the horseless carriage be hired at a cost of £25 half yearly, that Mr. Henry Tooms, a motor engineer who dwelt at Amiens Street in Dublin, be engaged as an instructor for a fee of ten shillings per lesson of two hours duration. This fee was very high in salary terms - the headmaster of the school, T. Clarke of Waverley Bray, who was an eminent Doctor of Literature was on an annual salary of a mere £100. And so ended the saga of one of Bray's earliest motor cars, soon its streets were to be adapted and changed for this rapid mode of transport.

I wonder what might have been if they had succeeded in building the car. Would they have built another one, followed by others and perhaps to-day Bray would be competing with Ford, Renault, Toyota and the rest? I think not but the thought is entertaining.

Let us go back further in time and have a look at an obscure figure whom most of you have never heard of, who was a visitor to Bray and who enjoyed walking along the beach, under the shadow of Bray Head, and admiring the splendid scenery which surrounds us.

Quinsboro Road

145

WILLIAM COBBETT

He was a famous person who had associations with Bray and he lived here for a short time, but yet was overlooked by local historians. Cobbett was born in England in 1763, the son of a farmer, and left home to join the army. Having served in the ranks in North America he returned to England, at the age of twenty eight, where he married. Shortly thereafter he went to France to see at first hand the aftermath of the Revolution and from there he sailed to America where he taught English to French émigrés and began a career as a writer under the strange name of 'Peter Porcupine'. He returned to Britain in 1800 and continued to write. Shortly after this he published a condemnation of British Administration in Ireland which resulted in his being charged with libel against the Lord Lieutenant and was fined a total of £1,000 (an astronomical sum in those days). Cobbett became a champion of the poor and continued to publish graphic descriptions of their distress and the abuses under which they were forced to live. In 1810 he was again in trouble, but this time it was more serious - the charge was 'sedition' and again he was found guilty and committed to Newgate Gaol where he was incarcerated for two years. 1817 saw his flight from England in order to avoid further persecution for his social and political essays, and he sought refuge in America where he lived for two years. An example of his writing, prompted by statements by the Prime Minister Peel who said that the Irish displayed symptoms of 'untameable ferocity, systematic guilt, systematic perjury and were in a state of depravity', was an article which he wrote addressed to the American people refuting such statements and arguing as follows:-

> ...Do you ever hear of this depravity, any of this untameable ferocity, on the part of these people ? You want no army, no extraordinary police, no suspension of ordinary laws to keep them in order....my belief is, that they have surpassed in success the emigrants from any other nation . And as to such of them with property or education they have certainly outstripped all others in the career of fame as well as prosperity. Does the salt air change their nature while they are crossing the seas?

Strange to relate that although Cobbett was always a strong advocate of Catholic Emancipation, an opponent of the cruel tithe system, outspoken in defence of the poor and the defender of the greater part of the Irish population that laboured under the most appalling injustice, he had never been to Ireland to see such misery for himself. This was to change. In the year 1834, at the age of seventy one, he arrived in Dublin and from there proceeded to stay near Bray in Shanganagh Castle as a guest of General Sir George Cockburn. He began to write letters to his home in Surrey describing what he saw here in Ireland.

> *I have this morning seen more than one thousand of working persons, men and women, boys and girls, all the clothes upon the bodies of all of whom were not worth so much as the frock smock that you go to work in..... there were about a hundred little girls in a school and about as many boys in another, neither had shoes or stockings, and the boys had no shirts........in another place I saw the most painful sight of all : Women, with heavy hammers, cracking stones into very small pieces, to make walks in gentlemen's gardens.*

A letter from Shanganagh Castle dated 10th November 1834, when Canon Alexander Roche was parish priest of Bray, reads:

> *I have learned that, when the charitable and most benevolent Catholic priests have contrived to collect a little money to give to poor creatures who are sick, or even in danger of dying ;.the poor creature is frequently obliged to give the bit of money to pay the rent of the place where he is, for fear of being flung into the street......a Catholic priest informed me, that he had just been to visit a sick man on his death bed, which was laid on a frame of old rough boards; man, ass, pig and family slept and had the dung heap in the same room.*

Cobbett toured Ireland and what he saw and found confirmed that he was correct in what he had written and said over the long years of his life. He quotes from the fifth chapter of St. James:

> *Go, you rich men, weep and howl for your miseries that will come upon you: the rust of your gold and silver shall eat your flesh as it were fire. You have by fraud kept back the hire of your labourers who have reaped down your fields; and their cries have entered into the ears of the Lord.*

Cobbett returned to his home in England and died shortly after, in 1835. Daniel O'Connell attended his funeral and followed the sad procession to the cemetery where he was laid to rest. And so ended the life of a most wonderful person, an Englishman, a Protestant and an Irish patriot. May he rest in peace.

1914-1918 WAR

Oh what a sad time this was for Bray. When I think of it, I especially remember the story of Gerald Palmer, a child who was in the Cripples Home here, and who lost his life together with 500 others when the ship bringing him to London was torpedoed just outside the Kish lighthouse. His memorial is a short sentence in the Home's minute book for October 1918. Gerard was, like most on board the Leinster, a non-combatant, but there were many soldiers on board returning to the front. The vessel was consequently a legitimate target, not much consolation to those who were killed! Many young men from Bray joined the British army, about eight hundred of them left from the railway station singing 'It's a long way to Tipperary' and 'Keep the home fires burning'. Among them were members of the Irish Volunteers who believed in promises given to John Redmond that Home Rule for Ireland would be granted after the conflict. There were soon to be two hundred mantelpieces with photographs of those who never returned, fading as the years grew longer and turning yellow with age. You have seen some of them. Another person I think of when I ponder on that terrible carnage is Tom Kettle, not a Bray man, but a member of the Volunteers like many who died, who expressed his feelings just before he was killed in his beautiful poem:

To My Daughter Betty The Gift of God

In wiser days, my darling rosebud, blown
To beauty proud as was your mother's prime,
In that desired, delayed, incredible time,
You'll ask why I abandoned you, my own,
And dear heart that was your baby's throne,
To dice with death. And, oh! they'll give you rhyme
And reason: some will call the thing sublime,
And some decry it in a knowing tone.
So here, while the mad guns curse overhead,
And tired men sigh, with mud for couch and floor,
Know that we fools, now with the foolish dead,
Died not for flag, nor King, nor Emperor,
But for a dream, born in a herdman's shed,
And for the secret Scripture of the poor.

Two hundred names and I suppose another two hundred others in some little town in Germany. These are the Bray ones:

148

Capt. Rev. Amar Acton	G.R. Allen	Richard Barrington
Lt. G. R. Bennet	W.D. Beatty	Thomas E. Boyd
W. Bookey	Thomas Brien	William Brien
Joseph Brien	Michael Brien	Phelim Brien
Thomas Bryan	James Breen	Pat Breen
Earnes Brabazon	H.W. Browne	William Brennock
Charles Brewster	William J. Byrne	James Byrne
Joseph Byrne	Martin Byrne	Patrick Byrne
Dominic Browne	Frank Caffrey	Neville Croome
R.E.Cusack	R. McCormick	G.B. Cream
Henry Craig	Alfred Cooper	John Cooling
John Connor	Wiliam Collins	Joseph Coffey
John Cleary	Maxwell Carpendale	A.R. Campbell
Denis Critchley	T. Crofton	Edward Dalton
Arthur Darley	Thomas Dornin	Thomas Dougherty
James Dowdall	James Doyle	John Doyle
John Darley	John Darlington	David Davies
Thomas Dawson	M. Day	E.N. Deane
Oliver Deane	F. Dobbin	William Doolan
T. Deane	R. Dobbin	Henry Donegan
Thomas Doolan	J. DeCourcy	Thomas Duffy
Eugene Duffy	A.C. Edwards	Austin Elmitt
George Elmitt	Patrick Flanagan	Thomas Flanagan
Michael Forde	J. Fraze	James Fitzpatrick
William Fitzpatrick	William Fox	William Fanning
Robert Farrell	Michael Fitzgerald	G.R. Gore
John Garvey	A. Gordon	A. St. J.Gore

George Gortham	R. McGregor Gow	Joseph Grantham
Edward Green	Henry Griffith	Eric Hamilton
W.S. Hughes	William Ham	Douglas Hamilton
N.F. Hone	Christopher Hickey	Henry Hayes
Michael Harney	Edwin Handcock	E.I. Hatte
Patrick Joyslinn	John Kitson	Frank Knox
Michael Kinsella	Thomas Kearns	William Kearns
Michael Kelly	William Kelly	Alfred Kelly
Patrick Kavanagh	Patrick Kelly	Patrick Kenna
Henry Stuart King	A. Kennedy	Patrick Kilduff
Albert Langridge	John Langton	P.J. Langton
Henry Lawrence	Joseph Lee	Robert Lee
George Lucas	John Ledwidge	J.E.Lowry
Henry John Malley	John Messitt	F.A.Marrable
Edward Murphy	Patrick Murphy	Thomas Murphy
John Murray	Richard Murray	M.A. Moses
William Mulvey	Arthur Meyer	Ernest Meyer
Patrick Mooney	John Martyr	Henry Mason
Douglas Maunsell	M.E. Moore	John Manly
John Madden	Thomas Mahony	Laurence Mc Call
J.A.Mc Mahon	R. McCormick	J.A.McCormick
Thomas McCormack	W.F.Mc Dowell	John McKenna
Alfred Mc Grego	Vivian McFarland	H.L. North
Bart Naylor	Robert Nicholson	James Nolan
Michael Nordell	Joseph O'Connor	Fred O'Donnell
George O'Reilly	James O'Reilly	Benjamin Pollard
Thomas Pattison	C.L. Price	Joseph Raverty

John Redmond	Patrick Reilly	Robert Revell
Edward Rice	J. V. Richards	H. Roberts
John Rogers	Thomas Sinnott	William Skelton
Algernon Smyth	John Sinnott	William Stedman
J. Strickland	Digby Sharkey	Francis Sherry
George Taylor	William Thompson	William Toole
J. St. J. Tredennick	Thomas Traynor	Patrick Toole
John Tiernan	C.H. Tisdall	Michael Toole
John Turner	James Tool	William Vance
J.C. Vanderkiste	Joseph Vance	Alexander Watt
Richard Waller	John Whitsitt	A.H. Wilson
Fitzharding Wintle		

You will find most of these names on the war memorial beside the Carlisle grounds (Bray Wanderers) near the station, and in Christ Church as well as on some of the pews in Holy Redeemer. In the beautiful little church (Church of Ireland) at Kilbride, there are two fine memorial windows. Republicans and Unionists, they died together.

A depressing subject. Let's look at something brighter for the moment !

ILLUMINATION IN BRAY

Up to the late 1850s, here in Bray we were all in the dark. The little bit of lighting that we had was scarce, and the insides of the houses at night were filled with dancing shadows reflected from the occasional candle with its flickering flame. The well-to-do had the luxury of an elegant oil lamp with a porcelain base beautifully painted in gay colours and a glass top. The streets at night were gloomy and silent, few ventured outside. The population was quiet and lived close to nature, just like the birds, they awoke at daybreak and retired at sundown.

It was different in Dublin because they had gas light, which first appeared on the streets in 1825; but then Dublin was a world away from us, and very few people in Bray had ever ventured that far. Things gradually changed and life here became very, very different.

The Bray Gas Company was set up in 1856, and within a few short years there were three lamps on the seafront, (the promenade hadn't been built yet), four on the Quinsboro Road, two on Seapoint Road, no doubt to light the way for sailors returning to their boats, and - wonder of wonders - the brilliant illumination of seventeen lamps on our Main Street. By the year 1864, when the American Civil War was still being fought with many Irishmen falling on both sides, a large gasometer behind the Harbour Bar had the capacity to provide the whole town with lighting, and by 1870 most of the buildings and large houses had gas lamps installed. (The gasometer was demolished a few years ago, and buried beneath it there was a metal box, a time capsule, within which were the names of those associated with its construction as well, as some coins of the period and other sundry items such as details of Bray's social and economic life at the time. I found no precious metal in it.)

Times were changing fast and soon there was the mind-boggling invention called electricity. Dublin had its first electric light bulbs in 1881, and soon its streets at night would become fashionable for an evening stroll. Bray was to follow shortly, and in 1896 The Bray Electric Light Works was firmly established, supplying the town with power that came from their generator at the brewery, which was known then as 'The Maltings'. Few homes had electricity until well into the first decade of the 20th century and it is interesting to read some of the contemporary notes about it. Father Colahan in April 1902 advised the Bray Technical Instruction Committee as follows:

from the start we should have a direct current dynamo and engine, also a storage battery and a complete set of commercial measuring instruments. A year hence, when alternating currents would have to be studied and the whole future of Electrical Engineering lies in this direction, the study of direct currents being merely introductory- we would have to provide apparatus for the generation, transformation, utilisation, measurement and general study of Electrical Energy in the form of single and two phase and three phase currents

The Technical School, then, hadn't got electricity and the committee, in September 1902, noted that when the school was to open on October 2nd that perhaps with a mild winter, heating other that that furnished by gas lighting might be unnecessary.

Down at the Harbour, although it wasn't built until the 1890's the area was always known as The Harbour, there were some unsatisfactory mooring facilities for boats that could no longer come up the river to the dock at Seapoint Road because of the building of the bridge which was to carry that new and rapid form of transport, the railway. There were many instances of seamen, returning to their berths in the dark, falling over the quay. Maybe the gloom was not fully to blame, perhaps a little bit of over-indulgence in liquid refreshment in the local hostelries might have been a contributory factor. All this was changed too, as when the new harbour was constructed, there were some lamps, and the lighthouse threw its first beam in 1897.

Thinking of those early days calls to mind Joe Bailey of Little Bray, who used to look after Bray Sea Anglers premises with Jim Toomey, and who lived to a ripe old age. His hands were badly blighted with some peculiar discolouration and scars. On enquiring as to what caused this, he said that when the electric cables were first being introduced to Bray, there was an appalling thunderstorm and a bolt of lightening struck the overhead heavy wires resulting in the insulation melting and dripping on Joe's hands as he passed underneath.

And now we have light everywhere, the brilliant display of colours along the Promenade in summer, the Christmas decorations on Main Street, the massive lamp standards with their underground cables. Our nights have been transformed into day by man's progress, but there remains a certain nostalgia for those evenings filled with shadows. Perhaps that is why the old oil lamps now occupy pride of place in our homes and modern imitations are made into electric lamps. Every house still has the very necessary candle in some drawer just for an emergency, and there's cause to light them a few times a year because of power cuts and fuses blowing. Outside in many sheds, there is a rusty storm lantern which someday just might be required. A beautiful custom prevails on Christmas Eve, but is regrettably fading slowly into the dim past, the candle in the window signifying a welcome within to the Holy Family on their lonely journey to a stable in Bethlehem.

Bibliography

Bovet, Marie Anne De, Three Months Tour in Ireland,Trans and condensed by Mrs Arthur Walter (London 1891).

Brewer, J.N. The Beauties of Ireland. (2 Vols. London 1826)

Concannon, Helena, Women of 'Ninety Eight (Dublin,1919)

Cullen, L.M. Princes and Pirates. The Dublin Chamber of Commerce 1783 1983 (Dublin, 1983).

Cullen, Brother Luke, Insurgent Wicklow. (Dublin, 1948)

Craig, Maurice, Dublin 1660-1860. (London, 1952; Dublin, 1969).

De Courcy ,Catherine, The National Gallery of Ireland.(Dublin, 1985).

David Dickson, The Gorgeous Mask, Dublin 1700 - 1850. (Dublin 1987).

Forde, Capt. Frank, The Long Watch. (Dublin, 1981).

Gaskin, James, Varieties of Irish History. (Dublin, 1869).

Grattan, Henry, Memories of the Life and Times of the Right Hon., Henry Grattan. (5 Vols., London 1839-'46).

Healy, Father James. Memories of Father Healy, of Little Bray.

Hall, Mr. & Mrs. 'Ireland'. (3 Vols., London 1841-3)

Holt, Joseph, Memoirs, of General J. Holt (2 Vols., London 1838).

Joyce, Weston St. John, The Neighbourhood of Dublin, (Dublin 1912).

Kee, Robert, The Green Flag, (London 1972).

Kettle, Thomas, The Days Burden, (Dublin 1910).

Large, Peter Somerville, Dublin. (London 1979).

Lewis, Samuel, A Topographical Dictionary of Ireland. (London 1837).

Madden, Richard, The United Irishmen, (2nd Ed., 4 Vols., Dublin 1858).

Mansfield, Charles, The Aravon Story, (Bray 1975).

Mason, St. Joh,. Prison Abuses in Ireland. (Dublin 1810).

Mc Murrow, Ann. Picnic In A Foreign Land.

Mills, Joseph. Recollections of Shankill.

O'Donnell, E.E. The Annals of Dublin. Fair City, (Dublin 1987)

O'Hanlon, John, Lives of the Irish Saints, (9 Vols., Dublin, London and New York, 1875-'99).

O'Hegarty, P.S, History of Ireland Under the Union, (London 1952).

O'Toole, P.L, History of the Clan O'Toole and other Leinster sects. (Dublin, London and New York, 1890).

Savage, John, Picturesque Ireland, (2nd. Ed.,New York, 1875-'99).

Scott, Rev. George Digby, The Stones of Bray. (Dublin 1913).

Tochnaye, Le Chevalier de La, A Frenchman's Walk Through Ireland, 1796-7 (Belfast 1917).

Turner, Kathleen, If You Seek Monuments: A Guide to the Barony of Rathdown (Dublin 1983).

Bray Catholic Monitor; Capuchin Annuals; Dublin Evening Post; Evening Mail; Freemans Journal; Illustrated London News; Irish Independent; Thom's Directories; Whitaker's Annual;

Index